# HORSE
# WATCHING

# HORSE
# WATCHING

## Desmond Morris

CROWN PUBLISHERS, INC., NEW YORK

Published in the United States of America in 1989
by Crown Publishers, Inc., 201 East 50th Street, New
York, New York 10022. Member of the Crown
Publishing Group.

Originally published in Great Britain in 1988 by
Jonathan Cape Ltd.

CROWN is a trademark of Crown Publishers, Inc.
Printed in the U.S.A.
Library of Congress Cataloging-in-Publication Data
Morris, Desmond.
    Horsewatching.
    1. Horses—Behavior—Miscellanea.   2. Horses
—Miscellanea.   I. Title.   II. Title: Horsewatching.
SF281.M67   1989        636.1          88-34019
ISBN 0-517-57267-2
20  19  18  17  16  15  14  13  12  11  10  9

# Contents

*v*

# HORSE
# WATCHING

# Introduction

If the dog is man's best friend, then the horse could be well described as man's best slave. For thousands of years horses have been harnessed, ridden, spurred, and whipped. They have been ruthlessly driven into the center of bloody battlefields where they have been hacked to pieces. For centuries they have toiled to drag heavy loads in the service of human ambition and then been rewarded at the end of their days with a trip to the glue factory. Their endless exploitation has been due to their amazing willingness to cooperate with their human companions and to struggle as best they can to please us. This temperament, which has so often been their undoing, stems from their naturally sociable life-style in the wild. Horses are by nature herd animals that live in small bands where cooperation is as powerful a theme as competition and where affection for one another is so strong that it is easily transformed into a horse-human bond. Unfortunately for the horse, this bond always ends with the human partner coming out on top, both literally

*1*

and metaphorically. Being so good-natured has cost the horse dearly.

The other side of the coin is man's great love and respect for the horse, now stronger than ever. For every example of brutality there are many cases of human devotion to horses, shown in long hours of selfless care and protection. For every callous horsewhipper today there is an army of passionate horse lovers, ready to rise at dawn and endure repeated hardships to ensure that their adored equines enjoy the best life-style possible. No animal is more admired or more highly valued.

What is it about the horse that awakens such intense feelings? Is it the animal's looks or its behavior, its graceful athleticism or its personality? The answer is to be found in a remark made nearly four hundred years ago by the naturalist Edward Topsel when he wrote of the horse that it possesses "a singular body and a noble spirit, the principal whereof is a loving and dutiful inclination to the service of Man, wherein he never faileth in Peace nor War . . . and therefore . . . we must needs account it the most noble and necessary creature of all four-footed Beasts." The clue to its special appeal is summed up by the words "noble and necessary." It is the combination of its proud bearing with its slavish service to man that makes it so irresistible. If it were noble but untamable, like a giraffe, we would wonder at its beauty but would not become passionate about it. If it were useful but ungainly, like a pig or a cow, we would be grateful for its services but would not, perhaps, compose poems to it or wax lyrical about its great spirit. No, the secret of equine appeal is that it slaves for us while still looking noble. It is our humble servant even though it has the demeanor of an animal aristocrat. The mixture is magical. If such a dignified beast is subordinate to our will, then we must indeed be masters of the world.

So it was, from the very start of equine domestication,

that man came under the spell of the horse. And right from the beginning there was one feature in particular that made a special impact on human affairs: its swift legs. Put to work for mankind, they gave a sudden boost to human expansion. For the first time our ancestors could move fast from place to place. Previously cattle had been the beasts of burden, the draught animals, and the pullers of the plow. Now they could be restricted to the slower, clumsier tasks, and the long-distance duties could be carried out more quickly by the horse. The mobility of man was magnified dramatically. Civilization could spread; trade routes could be opened up that were previously impossible. Cultural exchanges could be developed and the hybridization of ideas rapidly led to new creative vigor. For thousands of years, right up to the arrival of the internal combustion engine, the horse was the vehicle of the human conquest of the earth.

Its swift legs are significant, too, in having created its noble image. Because wild horses are fast-moving plains-living grazers, specialized for open country, they have had to evolve, over millions of years, the elegant frame of the muscle-rippling athlete. Rapid movement demands a certain style of body structure, a style that we, as athletes ourselves, appreciate. As a species we are fast runners, too—not diggers or climbers or clingers, but sprinters—and this gives us a common bond with the horse and a deeply rooted admiration for its amazing pace and grace. Psychologically it becomes an extension of our own running bodies. Sitting on its back we fuse with it in our minds to become one single, galloping, invincible being—the great centaur of ancient mythology.

When did all this happen? Surprisingly the horse was something of a latecomer on the domestic scene. Dogs, goats, sheep, and cattle had all been brought under human control for thousands of years when in the third millennium B.C. the horse was first domesticated. This took place in the area that is now southern Russia and northwest Asia, as part of the advancing tide of agricultural management. It was not, of course, mankind's first contact with the horse. Horses had been hunted for food since the Old Stone Age, as the beautiful prehistoric paintings on the cave walls of France and Spain testify, but there was then no attempt to bring them under control. They were trapped, speared, and eaten, and that was the limit of our relationship with them.

An intriguing sideline on this hunting phase is the fact that the number of wild horses was already decreasing without any help from humans. This was because at the end of the Ice Age there was a rapid spread of thick forests across most of the temperate zone. As an animal of the open plains, the horse was therefore losing ground little by little, and it is estimated that it might well have become extinct eventually had the ancient farmers not intervened and domesticated the species before it vanished forever. This is a pleasant reversal of the usual tale, in which human intervention condemns many a species to early retirement.

By the second millennium B.C. the decline of the horse had been turned around and as a domesticated animal it was once again spreading across Europe and increasing in numbers everywhere. By 1500 B.C. there were already two distinct types of domestic horse—the stocky ones of the colder northern regions and the slender ones of the warmer south. Specialization was beginning. From the heavyset northern ponies, by selective breeding, came the giant breeds that were to be the great beasts of burden in the farmers' fields and on the soldiers' battlegrounds. From the leggy southern horses came the magnificent Arab steeds that were later to father the modern Thoroughbreds of the racetrack. Wherever man explored and extended his range the horse went with him, until together they both acquired an almost global distribution. In the New World the Spanish intruders took a handful of horses with them—Columbus took thirty and Cortés sixteen—and before long these were to give rise to a whole new population of "Indian horses" and to change the social structure of the Plains Indians of the Americas.

As human populations everywhere began to explode into teeming millions, the number of horses thrown into service reached new heights. The whole of society seemed to be dependent on equine abilities, for farming, transportation, ceremony, sport and pleasure, and warfare. As weapons became more advanced, the fate of horses in times of war became more hideous. In a single day's fighting during the First World War seven thousand horses were killed. Of the million British horses sent to the front in that horrible conflict, only sixty-two thousand were ever to see British soil again. The majority of those that were lucky enough to escape the bombs and shells were rewarded after the armistice by being fed to prisoners of war or sold to continental farmers to be converted into fertilizer.

Despite the helplessness of horses in the face of the new weaponry, there was one final cavalry charge at the start of the Second World War. In 1939 the Polish cavalry rode bravely into battle against the tanks and dive-bombers of the Nazis. They were totally obliterated. The warhorse was gone forever. We who watch war films today are spared the horrors of equine bloodshed. Trained film horses are too valuable to be killed for our entertainment, and so their demise is merely suggested and we easily forget what a terrible price we have made the obedient horse pay for its domestication by man.

With the coming of the industrial revolution the age of the horse began to wane. First trains, and then automobiles, replaced the transportation horse. Finally, mechanized equipment swamped them out, both on the road and in the field. Trucks, tractors, tanks, buses, trains, vans, and family cars took over. The blacksmith became an endangered species. Only nostalgia kept the working horse alive. Apart from racing and leisure riding there was little for the modern horse to do. But with the removal of the arduous labor of earlier days came a growing respect and appreciation for our equine companions. Today, more than ever before, this respect is spreading with each generation. Equine commerce has been replaced by a much kinder equine love affair. For the first time in five thousand years it is once again a good time to be a horse. Man's best slave may not have been completely freed to roam the plains, but his slavery is now at least a benign one, full of care and devotion.

Back in the Elizabethan era, John Florio wrote, "England is the paradise of women, the purgatory of men, and the hell of horses." Today that hell has become something approaching a heaven for most of our horses, as we start to repay our long-standing debt to the noble beast. But strangely, even in our most zealous and enthusiastic infatuation with the horse we still fail to appreciate it for its own sake, as a remarkable species full of subtle expressions, body language, and social behavior. It is possible to be an expert horseman or horsewoman and still not fully comprehend the nature of equine social life. The bond between horse and rider dominates to the exclusion of horse-to-horse relations. *Horsewatching* fills this gap with some objective observations of one of our closest animal allies. And it ends with an examination of some of the less familiar aspects of horse myths and folklore. It is a book for horsewatchers everywhere, whether they have spent fifty years in the saddle or have never encountered a horse outside their television screens. After reading it I hope you will agree that the horse is, even today, a "noble and necessary" creature, which enriches all our lives merely by its presence among us.

# What Does a Horse Signal
# with Its Ears?

The ears of a horse are seldom still. Like radar dishes scanning the skies, they are forever moving this way and that, picking up tiny sound clues from the world around. For the wild ancestors of the domestic horse this was particularly important. Their only method of self-protection was fast retreat from danger and it was vital that they should be aware of the very first signs of trouble so that they could take off at high speed in the split second before a predator leapt to the attack. Their mobile ears were their early warning system.

Because the position of the ears varies as the horse's mood changes, its ear postures can be read as signals by its companions. One horse can tell the emotional condition of another by glancing at the way its ears are held or moved. So the ears have a double role—they receive sound signals and they transmit visual signals. The visual signals are unusually helpful because equine ears are so conspicuous. Other hooved animals, such as cattle, antelope, and deer, have horns or antlers protruding from the tops of their heads, which tend to hide their ear movements. But the ears of horses, not being obscured in this way, are highly visible even from a considerable distance, or when the animal can only be seen in silhouette. The language of equine ears is as follows:

When the ears are neutral they are held loosely upward, with their openings pointing forward and outward. In this way they scan the area in front of the horse and to either side of it. This basic posture provides the best coverage of the environment, but the moment a strange sound is heard, one or both ears rotate instantly to face it and examine it more carefully.

If a sound appears to be strange or worrying, the horse also turns its head or even its whole body toward the source and then pricks its ears so they are stiffly erect with their apertures facing directly toward the sound. *Pricked ears* are typical of horses that are startled, vigilant, alert, or merely interested and are most commonly seen during frontal greetings.

The opposite of pricked ears are *airplane ears.* Here they flop out laterally with their openings facing down toward the ground. These are the ears of a tired or lethargic horse or one that has completely lost interest in the world around it—they indicate clearly that the animal is psychologically at a low ebb. Sometimes the posture becomes more extreme and there is a *drooped ears* posture, with the ears hanging down loosely on either side of the head. This is seen when a horse becomes very dozy or is in actual pain and wants to switch off all incoming messages. These sideways ear postures are also used as signals of inferiority during status battles or stressful social encounters. The weak horse is saying, "I am not arguing with you, I have switched off, you are the boss, so now leave me alone."

Sometimes it is possible to observe a ridden horse adopting *drooped backwards ears* as a special signal. The ears are stuck out sideways, but their openings are directed backward toward the rider. This indicates a horse that is submissive toward and fearful of its human companion. The lateral element of the ear posture reveals the submissiveness and the twisting backward of the apertures shows the animal's need to catch any tiny sound from the fear-inducing figure on its back. This ear posture is common in horses with brutal owners. It is also observed when male and female horses encounter one another in a sexual mood. The female often adopts this position of the ears when her strong sexual urges make her approach a powerful stallion. She is attracted to him, but at the same time is rather fearful of him and signals this with her ears. For him, the submissiveness of her ear signals acts as a positive sexual stimulant and reassures him that he is not about to be dealt a savage kick as he approaches her from behind.

If ordinary fear turns to blind panic, alert ears return. They are more erect now but at the same time they are busily twitching and flicking. A horse with *flicking ears* may well be on the verge of bolting in terror.

At the opposite end of the emotional scale, where anger, aggression, and dominance rear their heads, there is the characteristic *pinned ears* signal in which the horse flattens its ears back against its head so that they almost disappear from view. In silhouette, an angry horse looks quite earless and it has been suggested that one of the reasons why humans can control horses so easily is that we must always appear dominant and ferocious to them simply because our own ears are forever pinned to the sides of our heads. In horse language this must make us seem very intimidating indeed, and there is nothing they can do—it must seem to them—to change our domineering mood. No matter how submissively they behave, we never prick up our ears in a greeting, or flop them out sideways in dozy subordination.

There is a good reason for the pinned ear signal being

the most aggressive. It is derived from the primeval horse's "ear protection" posture employed to keep ears as safe as possible from the attacks of rivals. Tucked back they are least likely to be bitten or torn, and during the course of evolution that old self-defense posture has become part of everyday equine body language. Instead of being reserved purely for moments of actual fighting, it is now employed as a threat signal when two rival horses encounter one another. The aggressive animal simply pins back its ears, saying in effect, "If you want a fight I am ready for one," and the other horse can then either act submissively or threaten back. In this way disputes can often be settled without recourse to serious fighting, the displays usefully replacing the bites and kicks.

In one special context there are two unusual ear reactions. If a racehorse is drugged, its condition is most clearly revealed by the odd way in which its ears behave. If it has been given a depressant, its ears droop out sideways and do so even when it is otherwise active. When it walks, these drooping ears may flop up and down, as though they are no longer being operated by the ear muscles. If the drugged horse has, on the other hand, been given stimulants, its ears then go completely rigid. In these two situations it is possible to have one's suspicions aroused when a particular horse behaves oddly before a race.

Finally, it must always be remembered that during a horse's daily life its ears (in normal, undrugged animals) are constantly moving to pick up new sounds. Mobile ears, turning this way and that, are, by their very activity, signals of shifting attention and interest. Companion horses can quickly note the way in which another member of the herd has become curious about something in the distance in a particular direction. Then they too can home in with their listening devices. These shifts in direction can override other considerations. If a noise is coming from behind, the ears will be rotated backward regardless of the general mood of the animal. Only when these listening actions have died down will the ears revert to their quieter, long-term "mood posture." Horses are quick to learn the differences between short-term attention signals and long-term mood signals, and it is easy enough for us to do the same. Once we have learned this simple "language" of the equine ears, it will help us to tell at a glance the emotional state of our animals and begin to enter their world more intimately.

# How Well Can Horses Hear?

Better than we can. Their highly sensitive ears can detect a wider range of sounds, from very low frequency to very high, and at all levels they have more acute hearing.

Adult humans have the ability to hear sounds up to about 20,000 cycles per second, but this sinks to 12,000 by the time we are in our sixties. Tests on horses have established that they can hear up to 25,000 cycles, appreciably above our range, but as with us this starts to decline with age.

The acuity of their hearing exceeds ours thanks to their large and wonderfully mobile external ears. Controlled by no fewer than sixteen muscles, each ear can be rotated about 180 degrees, pinpointing the source of particular sounds from a great distance. Time and again a horse owner has noticed that his horse has reacted to an approaching noise before he himself could detect anything.

Horses are so good at detecting natural disturbances such as distant storms, high winds, and earthquakes that some horsemen have insisted that their animals possess a sixth sense. To be certain of this, however, it would be necessary to study the reactions of a totally deaf horse. The chances are that in all such "mysterious" reactions the horses are in reality responding to tiny sounds that are still too far away for the human ear. Even earthquakes may be sensed in this way because they are preceded by low-frequency geophysical vibrations that could be heard at the lower end of a horse's hearing range. People living in earthquake zones have frequently noted that their steeds become intensely agitated and highly vocal just before a quake strikes—a useful early warning for insensitive humans.

These comments should not be taken to mean that horses necessarily lack a sixth sense, but merely that we should be wary of assuming that such a sense is operating if we observe an equine reaction that is inexplicable to us. However, it is possible that if we could eliminate all the normal senses of sound, sight, smell, taste, and touch, we might well find that, like many other species, the horse is able to respond to such clues as the changing magnetic field of the earth. Many riders, thrown by their horses during an afternoon ride, have marveled at the way their animals have unerringly found their way back home, over strange terrain, later that night. Such cases may be examples of sensitive hearing—the twisting ears of the animal picking up distant, familiar sounds—or they may be examples of even more extraordinary sensitivity to the "magnetic map" of the home territory. Whichever sense is operating, one thing is certain: Horses are remarkably finely tuned to the environment in which they live.

Such is this sensitivity that a particularly noisy environment can be distressing to a horse. People who keep their animals near airports or busy road systems report that they often become high-strung. What for us would be an unpleasant cacophony of sounds must rise to an unbearable din for the horses. They can shut out the sounds to some extent by flattening their ears, but even this is not enough and care should be taken to avoid such locations wherever possible. Police and parade horses have to be schooled into the highly unnatural response of *not* reacting to shouts, cheers, drums, and bands on public or ceremonial occasions and this requires a great deal of patience and training. Even when they have had their natural reactions suppressed in this way they can be observed to wince and twitch as the blasts of sound hit them. They may not rear up or flee in panic as they wish to do, but they still show by their telltale body language that they are far from calm as their delicate ears are bombarded with painful stimuli.

One special benefit of the horse's sensitivity to sound is that an intelligent rider can readily train a horse to respond to softly spoken, simple words of command. Any horse can be made to react, just like a dog, to words such as "stop," "go," "yes," and "no"—and many others—but for some reason this ability is not utilized to the full. Some horsemen seem to feel, misguidedly, that it is wrong to talk to a horse and that all commands should be given by physical means—tugging, pulling, twisting, and the rest—but such an attitude fails to make use of one of the horse's great attributes—its brilliant sense of hearing.

# How Many Sounds Does a Horse Make?

The vocal repertoire of the horse is not great and the sounds it can make are far from musical, but it nevertheless possesses a simple, useful language of snorts and squeals, neighs and nickers, which convey its changing moods to its companions. There are eight main sounds:

## 1. The Snort

This carries the message "There may be danger here." It is performed by a horse experiencing a conflict between curiosity and fear. It detects something that arouses its interest, but which makes it slightly wary. The snorting reaction does two things simultaneously: It clears the animal's respiratory passage, ready for action, and it also alerts the other members of the herd to the possibility of danger. Because the snorting horse faces the possible threat, the sound acts as an indicator of the direction from which the threat is coming, allowing the other horses to focus on it as well. In a sense it is the equine equivalent to the much louder canine bark. The snorting horse, unlike the barking dog, can only be heard from a distance of about 50 yards. This means that if it has spotted something worrying in the far distance, it can alert its companions without revealing the presence of the herd to what may be a prowling predator.

The snort is a powerful exhalation of air through the nose, with the mouth held shut. It lasts between 0.8 and 0.9 seconds and has an audible fluttering pulse created by the vibrations of the nostrils. The head is usually held high, as is the tail, with the whole body of the horse showing a state of high excitement and readiness for fleeing.

Although its most common use is when a strange object is detected in the distance, it is also frequently employed when one stallion challenges another. Again the mood is one of great interest tinged with anxiety—a state of conflict.

## 2. The Squeal

This is a defensive signal. In aggressive encounters it means "Don't push me any further," and suggests to the rival that if it fails to desist, retaliation will be provoked. A lactating mare that has sore nipples and resents being touched will also squeal as a protest. And a flirting mare being approached by a stallion will object to his advances with this same sound. In all cases the squeal acts as a protest signal, saying, "Stop it!" However, in sexual encounters it sometimes has an added nuance, the message then being "Stop it, I like it!"

Squeals vary considerably in intensity. They may be as short as 0.1 seconds, or as long as 1.7 seconds. At full strength they may be heard up to 100 yards away. Some of the loudest squeals are heard during encounters between stallions and mares. Squealing is usually performed with a closed mouth, but sometimes the corners of the mouth may open slightly.

### 3. The Greeting Nicker

This is a low-pitched, guttural sound with a pulsating quality that is employed as a friendly "come here" signal. It is used at close quarters, once the companion has been recognized, and can be heard at up to 30 yards. It is given when one horse greets another one in a welcoming fashion, and it is also commonly heard at feeding time, when it is given to the human companion bringing the food. In such cases it has been called a "begging" sound, but it is really more of a general salutation—the horse is saying in effect, "Hello, good to see you!"

### 4. The Courtship Nicker

Performed by a stallion approaching a mare, this is also a greeting, but with a specifically sexual flavor. The human equivalent would be something like "Hello, beautiful!" As the stallion performs this nicker, he often nods his head vigorously, keeping the mouth shut and the nostrils wide open. This kind of nicker is longer, lower, and more broken up into syllables. Different stallions have different pulse rates in their courtship nickers, so that it should be possible for the female to identify the approaching male without even looking at him.

### 5. The Maternal Nicker

This is given by a mare to her foal and is very soft, barely audible from a distance. It is used when the mare is mildly concerned about her offspring's safety and the gentle, intimate message is "Come a little closer." Foals react to this sound from birth, without any learning process. In fact, it is possible to get a newborn foal to follow a human simply by imitating this sound, so compulsive is its response to it.

## 6. The Neigh

Sometimes called the whinny, this sound starts out as a squeal and then ends as a nicker. It is the longest and loudest of horse calls, lasting an average of 1.5 seconds and being audible over half a mile away. This is the equine equivalent of the canine howl, given when one horse becomes isolated from its group, or when it spots one of its companions in the distance. Usually the call is answered, the messages being something like "I am over here, is that you?" and "Yes, it's me, I hear you." It helps to keep a group together or at least to maintain contact at a distance. Experiments have revealed that horses react more strongly to the neighing of members of their own groups than to strange horses. And mares are more responsive to their own foals than to other young horses. This proves that each neigh is learned as belonging to a particular individual and is a means of personal identification. Listening closely to different neighs it soon becomes clear that they do in fact each have their own special quality. There are even breed differences in addition to individual ones. And it is possible to tell a male neigh from a female one by the little grunt that stallions add at the ends of their calls. Some people erroneously believe that neighing or whinnying is a sign of fear and panic, but this is a complete misunderstanding. It is a request for information, not a cry of alarm.

## 7. The Roar

When horses are fighting seriously and are in a savagely emotional mood—it may be intense fear, intense rage, or both at once—they can be heard to roar or, at a higher pitch, to scream. These sounds are rarely heard in domestic horses unless they are running wild in a natural herd or are being kept in a large breeding group—not a common occurrence where modern horse management is concerned.

## 8. The Blow

This is like a snort without the pulsations or fluttering quality in the noise. It is a simple exhalation of air through the nose and carries a similar message to the snort, but with less tension. The blow may say, "What's this?" but sometimes it appears to be simply a signal of well-being, saying no more than "Life is good!"

In addition, horses may be heard to grunt and groan with exertion or boredom, sigh occasionally, and snore loudly, but these are of minor significance in their vocal repertoire. In truth, the horse does not have a very elaborate language of sounds and does not use them in a rigid manner. Not one of them is confined to a single context with a single message. Although "typical" messages have been given here, each sound can be heard in a whole variety of situations, where other elements of the social event alter its precise meaning. Equine vocalizations should always be "read" with this in mind.

# What Does a Horse Signal with Its Tail?

A horse's tail rises and falls like a needle on a dial that registers excitement. A tail held high signifies alertness, activity, and exuberance. One drooped low indicates sleepiness, exhaustion, pain, intense fear, or submission.

The reason for this is that the faster the horse accelerates as it moves forward, the more its "antigravity" muscle system goes into action. These muscles help to lift it up and along, and the raising of the tail is part of this process. When the horse decelerates, putting on the brakes, the reverse occurs and the tail is pressed low. These ancient connections between up-and-go and down-and-stop have been "borrowed" to provide special signals for equine body language. A horse may raise or lower its tail purely as a signal now, without even moving its body.

A boisterous young horse, for example, may approach another and show its readiness for play by flicking its tail high up over its back—as fully raised as is anatomically possible. Sometimes the tail may even curl right over its back, so intense is the "lift" when initiating play. This invitation signal is immediately understood by another young horse and a game quickly begins. The key point here

*21*

is that, at the moment of tail-raising, the animal inviting play may not have been accelerating. It may even have been stationary. Up-and-go has here been transformed into up-and-"let's go." The movement of the tail is no longer *caused* by acceleration, it has become symbolic of it. It has become, as it were, a request for acceleration: "Let's dash off and play together."

In a similar way, a tail can be drooped by a stationary horse as a signal saying, "I am tired and weak, I submit to you, you are the boss." If acutely afraid of another horse, an animal may even tuck its tail tight against its rear end, almost like a dog trying to "put its tail between its legs."

If a horse becomes very aggressive or tense then another tail signal is a stiffening of the fleshy base of the tail, so that it tends to stick out behind the animal more than usual, as if it were a hairy rod.

In sexual encounters, the tails of both stallions and mares are held high because of the excitement of the moment, but there is a small difference, namely that the female's tail is also held over to one side as a sexual invitation signal, while it is kept in the raised posture.

In addition to the up-and-down signals of the tail, there are also rapid swishing movements, in various directions. These are derived from irritation responses when a horse is troubled by insects and other pests. The tail in this context is being used essentially as a fly switch, but equine body language has borrowed this primeval action, as it has others, for use in social encounters. An anxious, frustrated, or confused horse may flick its tail this way and that, first sideways, then vertically, then around in an arc, signaling its irritation. The "fly" at which its tail is swishing has become symbolic. The source of the annoyance is now psychological rather than physical. In dressage contests this tail-wagging can cause a loss of points for what is termed "resistance"—in other words it is taken as a sign that the horse is ill at ease and therefore badly prepared by its rider.

When a horse becomes particularly angry, it may express its mood by increasing the power of the tail-swish, delivering a side flick so strong that the tail hairs actually whistle through the air and can even draw blood if they strike human flesh. Or it may flick its tail high in the air and then slap it down hard. Clues such as these often herald a savage kick, as the horse's bad temper grows.

In some countries the illegal use of a whip equipped to give an electric shock produces a highly characteristic tail reaction. As the horse is "buzzed" it stiffens the base of its tail, swings the tail around in a rapid circle, then lifts it high in the air and slaps it hard down on its rear end. This is all done in the space of a second, but it is a vital telltale clue that an illegal piece of goading has taken place.

Another, bizarre form of cheating has been uncovered in the case of the high-stepping Tennessee Walkers. These all-too-often brutalized horses may have their own tails docked and then false tails fitted over the stumps in an exaggeratedly erect posture, to give them that excited, high-tail look. Sometimes, as an alternative, a piece of ginger is inserted in the unfortunate horse's anus, to produce a similar effect. That familiar old expression from countless Western movies, "Let's hightail it out of here," has somehow lost its innocence.

# What Does a Horse Signal
# with Its Neck?

The horse's long and powerful neck gives it the ability to move its head about with considerable flexibility. This provides it with a variety of head and neck signals that can operate as useful clues to its changing moods. Some of these actions are derived from cleaning movements. Horses suffer terribly from flies and other insect pests that buzz around their faces, and they frequently make a short sharp movement of the neck as a way of disturbing and possibly driving away these small tormenters. The most popular version is the *head shake,* a vigorous sideways action that quickly sets up a cloud of flies. Another is the upward *head toss,* and a third is the up-and-back movement of the *head jerk.* The primary role of these actions may be self-comforting, but they also exist in a secondary, social form. Whenever a horse is irritated by the actions of a companion, be it equine or human, it is likely to reveal its frustration and annoyance by behaving as though it is being tormented by insect pests. Tossing, shaking, or jerking its head, it signals its annoyance even in the complete absence of any real insects. This is the equine equivalent of a human scratching the back of his head when he is angry. Like horses we

*24*

perform a primitive "irritation reaction" to a new form of irritation that is now completely in the mind. The people who infuriate us are not actually stinging the skin on top of our heads and yet we behave as if they are.

These tossing and shaking actions must not be confused with *head bobbing*, in which the horse ducks the head down and back repeatedly. This is usually the animal's way of increasing its range of vision and improving its understanding of objects directly in front of it. The *head wobble* is another head movement with a very distinct meaning. In this, the nosetip of the head is twisted from side to side while the top of the head stays more or less still. It is as if the animal is clearing its head, and its message is "I am ready for action." In a curious way it is almost self-congratulatory, and there is a "cocky" head sway seen among humans that has both a similar form and a similar meaning.

Forward movements of the head, such as *head thrusting, head lunging*, and *nose nudging*, are all self-assertive actions. The thrust and the lunge are aggressive movements related to biting, but the nudge, performed with the top of the nose and with the mouth closed, is a milder display and says little more than "Hey, what about me?" or "Come on, let's get on with it." It demands attention and is used both to horse and to human companions. Sometimes it is used to gain interest when a horse is in acute discomfort and is an action that should never be ignored if the cause of it is not fully understood.

If a horse wishes to signal that it is trying to avoid something it will swing its head away from the source of unpleasantness. A quick twist of the neck, in retreat as it were, tells a companion that the horse finds something distasteful, whether it be a direct physical contact or some symbolic intrusion. *Head snaking* (as distinct from head shaking) is a curious side-to-side wobble of an outstretched neck, seen when a dominant stallion is having trouble rounding up his wandering mares. The darting movements of the head were initially bite threats but during evolution they have become stylized as the rhythmic wobble of the head snake. Now today a stallion has only to perform this action for his mares to understand what it is he demands of them.

Finally, there are a few rather disturbing neck movements that crop up occasionally. These include the strange *neck wringing* movement in which the whole neck is twisted dramatically this way and that. It is employed in playful interactions as a way of saying, "I want to go in all different directions at once," but it is also seen in more serious contexts where its message is an unhappy one: "I want to get out of here." Even worse are the stereotyped actions that some horses perform for hours on end as a way of relieving the boredom of isolation in small stalls. These include repeated *weaving* actions similar to those seen in parrots and various other caged animals that wish to escape but cannot do so, and *head circling* movements that make one dizzy to watch. Any such neck movement that persists for long periods of time indicates that the animals' environment is oversimplified and needs enriching in some way. These are actions that are never observed in wild animals, and this alone should alert us to the fact that something is wrong with our animal husbandry wherever they occur.

# What Does a Horse Signal with Its Body?

The bearing of a horse tells a great deal about its mood. Generally speaking, the more elevated its posture the more excited the horse. As the animal becomes increasingly aroused, its whole body seems to grow taller and more impressive. The head is held high and the tail stands up proudly. By contrast, as the horse becomes less excited and eventually drowsy, bored, or submissive, its head and tail slump low and its body sags down, making the animal appear smaller. This vertical display—from liveliness to lifelessness—is clearly understood by its companions, who respond accordingly. It is part of the body language of horses, employed every time they meet.

Only when the level of excitement reaches a point where they set off at a full gallop does this vertical rule break down. Then the physical demands of high-speed locomotion force the horse's body into a sleeker, more horizontal posture despite the very high level of arousal.

In addition to general muscle tone there are three characteristic body signals that can be read with ease: They are the *body check*, the *shoulder barge*, and the *rump presentation*.

The body check is employed by a dominant animal that wants to impede the movement of a rival. It is a form of threat, saying, "I am in charge." The intimidator swings its body across the front of the other horse and prevents it from advancing. This puts the checked animal in something of a dilemma. It can either react to the challenge and try to force its way forward, or it can simply allow itself to be controlled, standing meekly where it is or turning away and moving off. If it retreats in this situation it is admitting defeat and recognizing the body checker as its superior. This is because the act of turning away is a specific signal, the equivalent of throwing in the towel, employed by horses during an actual fight. The action of the body checker forcing its rival to stand its ground or actively demonstrate its inferiority is therefore a convenient way of reinforcing high status without necessarily resorting to dangerous fighting. The disadvantage of real fighting, even if you are the stronger animal, is that you may sustain an injury during the course of defeating your weaker rival. In the wild, such an injury might make all the difference between escaping from a predator and being caught and killed, and so any system that can settle disputes by display rather than by physical violence is favored.

The shoulder barge is a more intense version of the body check, with the threatening animal carrying the display further, so that it makes contact with its rival and pushes into it. If this fails to intimidate the other animal, it may then be necessary to escalate the encounter to the level of a real fight, with displays giving way to violent physical action, but this is always a last resort.

One of the reasons why there are so many "objections" and "steward's inquiries" at racetracks is because if a jockey deliberately urges his mount to shoulder barge a rival horse, the latter is not merely impeded but also psychologically intimidated by the action, responding to it as though it is the gesture of an aggressive, dominant animal. This has the effect of slowing it up more than might be expected from the simple "bumping" it receives. On the polo field precisely the same action is employed deliberately as an accepted element of the sport, a good polo pony being the one that is ready and willing to shoulder barge all comers and never to be intimidated by such contacts.

The rump presentation is employed as a defensive display. The horse in question simply swings around so that its rump is offered to its rival. This is a more guarded form of threat and says, "Stop annoying me or I will kick you." In origin it is a lining-up of the body for a backward kick and acts as a warning sign of a possible attack to come, should the other horse not keep its distance. In behavior terms it is what is called an "intention movement," because with it the animal signals its intention of making a vigorous action. Other horses quickly learn to read the preparatory stages of the action and respond to them without waiting for the rest of the movement to follow. In this way a rump display becomes an efficient substitute for a full rear-kicking action.

# What Does a Horse Signal with Its Legs?

There are several leg signals used by horses to show their changing moods. One is *pawing the ground*. This is a scraping action of one front leg in which the foot is dragged backward. In origin it is a feeding movement or a way of investigating the ground beneath the feet. It may be used to scratch beneath the surface or to test its resistance. On such occasions it is purely mechanical and does not act as part of equine body language, but it may also be employed emotionally in a nonmechanical way by frustrated horses that have a strong urge to move forward. If something prevents them from advancing—either a fear of doing so or a physical obstruction—then they may start to paw at the ground as a way of expressing their thwarted feelings.

The *front-leg lift* is a threat. It is a mild version of the forward strike employed when horses attack one another frontally. If two stallions are doing battle they may both rear up on their hind legs and strike out with their front legs. The leg lift is simply a way of saying, "This is what I will do to you if you provoke me further," and is the equine equivalent of the human fist shake.

The *back-leg lift* is a more defensive threat acting as a

signal that a full-blooded kick is on the way if matters get worse. It is used to amplify the rump presentation signal if that has failed to have the desired effect. It is sometimes employed by mares that wish to repel their overattentive foals. If the foals are being a nuisance and persist in searching for the udder at times when the mare does not want to feed them, she will drive them away with a firm lift of whichever hind leg is nearer to them.

*Knocking* and *stamping* are two other ways in which horses can signal that they are in a mildly threatening mood. Again, both actions are related to kicking, but in a highly modified form. Knocking consists of a raising and lowering of a hind leg in such a way that it makes a forcible tapping sound on the ground. Stamping is a similar up-and-down movement performed with one of the front feet. Knocking and stamping are used in contexts that can best be described as "mild protest." A mare may knock when her foal is irritating her. A riding horse may stamp as a protest when it is being saddled up for a journey it does not want to make. Like other body signals, these actions are directed not only toward other horses but also at human companions, who—consciously or unconsciously —soon learn to read the signs.

# How Expressive Is a
# Horse's Face?

The subtle and complex body language of the horse involves various facial expressions, not as elaborate as those of human beings but still able to convey many shifting moods and emotions.

The earliest expression seen in a young foal is one called "snapping." In this the animal opens its mouth, draws back the corners of its mouth, and then, with teeth exposed, starts to open and shut its jaws. Sometimes the teeth make contact and sometimes they just fail to do so. When they do snap together there is a clapping noise—some authors have called this action "teeth-clapping." Others have stressed the opening and closing of the jaws and have christened it "jaw-waving." Its function is submissive and the message is "I am only a little foal and I mean you no harm so please don't hurt me." It is performed toward any large or strange horse that comes close. By the time the young horses are three years old the action has almost ceased and its role in equine social life is clearly to protect the weak newcomers to the herd.

The curious feature of snapping is that at first glance it looks as though it is slightly aggressive—as if the young animal is making biting movements. But the older horses do not make this human error in interpretation, and they respond to it for what it is in horse language—a stylized grooming signal. When two horses meet they often express their friendliness by mutual grooming—each nibbling the other's mane or some other part of the coat. Such mutual aid is only possible when there is no tension or threat between the two animals. Making a movement as if to start grooming therefore has about it a highly nonaggressive flavor. The young foal, by making a mock grooming movement with its mouth, is able to say in horse language, "I am friendly," and in that way escape any hostility from adults.

The exact opposite of this snapping mouth is when the jaws are held tensely open with the teeth fully exposed. This is the true bite threat used in fighting as a warning of an imminent attack. It is often enough to scare off an opponent without actual contact being made. At a less violent moment, a horse's tense aggression is shown by a tight-lipped mouth. Other forms of tension, such as fear, anxiety, and pain, are also accompanied by a stiff mouth, in contrast with the relaxed lips of a peaceful animal or one that is exhausted. When a horse is sleepy it often lets its lower lip droop and sag down.

When sexually active, a stallion often shows the strange expression that is known as the "*flehmen* face." He does this in response to the smell of the mare's urine, curling up his top lip to expose the upper teeth and gums. He stretches his head forward as he does this and appears to be sniffing the air with great intensity. The movement and expression show his great interest in the fragrance of the female. Occasionally a strange-smelling chemical will set off this reaction and then it can be seen in the mare as well as the stallion. Sometimes a female horse will perform the *flehmen* face in response to the urine of another female,

*33*

and so the name "stallion face" sometimes used for this expression is a little misleading, although it is certainly true that stallions are more prone to show it.

Nostrils can be wrinkled in disgust by horses just as by humans, and like us they flare them when in a state of excitement or intense emotion. Because Arab horses have nostrils that appear flared all the time (as part of their desert-breathing specialization) they give the impression of always being more alert and excited than other breeds.

The eyes of a horse are usually closed when it is in pain or exhausted, opened wide with fear, anxiety, and apprehension, half-closed in peaceful relaxation and submission, and looking back in anger. The angry eye shows some white, as the eyes bulge and turn backward, but it is a mistake to think that every horse that is showing a little white in its eye is in fact hostile. It can simply be looking behind at something of special interest.

# How Good Is a Horse's Sense of Smell?

One of the most characteristic features of a horse is its long face. This elongation is not just a matter of making space for the big grinding teeth. It also provides a housing for the extensive nasal cavities. It has been claimed that their complex, convoluted passages are equal in area to the whole outer body surface of a horse, and it is clear that horses are superior to humans when it comes to sniffing the morning air. They can detect important smells wafting in from the far distance—something completely beyond the capabilities of their owners.

Smell is significant to wild horses in several major contexts. They must be able to identify the odor of a hungry predator that may be lurking in cover or attempting to creep up on a grazing herd. They must be able to pinpoint the presence of life-saving, faraway water holes. And male horses must be able to tell when a distant mare is coming into heat.

Horse owners have often noticed that a stallion, even when confined inside a stable, can smell the irresistible fragrance of a sexually receptive mare who, unseen, is pacing up and down in some remote field. So keen is the stallion's sense of smell in this context that he can detect such a mare at distances of up to half a mile. Aiding him in this feat is the special *flehmen* action, in which he inhales deeply, then curls his top lip upward so that it closes off his nostrils. This has the effect of trapping the female-fragrant air inside his nasal cavities and forcing it to circulate deeply there. As part of this cavity system there are specialized pits called "vomeronasal organs," or "Jacobsen's organs," which are particularly efficient at detecting details of animal scent signals, or pheromones. These pheromones tell the deep-sniffer not only the sexual condition and emotional state of the signaler, but also make it possible for one horse to identify another one personally and individually.

This personal identification system can be observed in action whenever two horses meet for the first time. Eager to establish social contact, each horse sniffs the other with extreme care. In particular they smell one another's breath. They do this by coming close together and standing nose to nose. One of them then blows into the other's nostrils, sending its personal "calling card" into the sensitive nasal cavities, where it is read and memorized. Then the second animal offers a reciprocal snort. Now each animal has presented itself for consideration and, if they are friendly to one another, a rapport between them will be initiated.

Some human horse owners have insisted that they too can become closer to their animals by blowing into their nostrils in precisely the same way. They claim that after an exchange of snorts, nose to nose with one of their favorite horses, the bond between them is far closer than it was before. They argue that this is an almost magical way of developing a deep intimacy with an equine companion. Where the horse in question has a friendly disposition and where the human involved has behaved well toward the animal, this may be true. Their friendship may well become stronger. But it is worth remembering that when this type of greeting is performed between wild horses under natural conditions it does not always lead to deep friendships. It is almost as likely to lead to savage fights, as two animals try to establish relative dominance. If the greeters, on sniffing one another, discover that they are potential rivals, then all that the blowing and sniffing will do is to identify the opponent and to keep him or her indelibly engraved in the memory, for future reference. For the more kindly and loving horse owners this should not, however, pose a problem. For them, a mutual nose blow will be as good as a fond embrace.

One of the problems arising from a stallion's ability to sniff a sexy mare from great distances is that it puts him off other important matters, such as winning races or taking part in great parades in an orderly fashion. Stallion owners faced with this difficulty have been forced to resort to dirty tricks to disrupt the natural behavior. The simplest solution, it would appear, is to smear the insides of the stallion's nostrils with strong-smelling aromatic oils. These mask the scent of the mare and, for that matter, most other odors, and keep the stallion's mind on the business in hand. There are pitfalls in this method, however, because using such powerful substances inside the highly sensitive nostrils can cause distress and may damage the membranes if it is done inexpertly.

Mares with foals employ scent as a primary method of identifying their own offspring and distinguishing them from those of other females. This has been proved by tests that eliminated the possibility of visual or voice clues being used. It does not mean that a mare is actually incapable of identifying her own foal by its appearance or its voice, but simply that in the dark when all is quiet she can still sniff out her young one. Observers of wild horses have noticed the way that the mares keep on sniffing their foals, day after day, repeatedly checking their scent qualities. This is presumably because, as they grow older, the personal fragrance of the foals changes slightly, as does their appearance, and the mothers feel the need to keep well up-to-date.

In matters of taste, as distinct from smell, horses have the usual four responses: bitter, sweet, salt, and sour. In this respect their reactions appear to be similar to ours, except that they have a greater tolerance for bitter substances— foods that we would find unbearably bitter are happily consumed by horses. They are certainly capable of developing a sweet tooth, as any horse owner knows, with a special passion for sugar lumps and peppermints. Interestingly these cravings are not so strongly developed in very young horses and it may well be that the older animals like the sweet objects not so much because of their taste but because of the friendly interactions and the special, rewarding moments between horse and rider that they represent.

# How Well Can Horses See?

The strangest feature of the horse's eye is its huge size—twice as big as the human eye. It is one of the largest in the entire animal kingdom and amazingly is bigger than the eye of either the elephant or the whale. It also possesses a special light-intensifying device—the *tapetum lucidum*—which is a layer that reflects light back onto the retina and makes the horse much better than its rider at seeing in dim light. It also gives the horse's eye a "glow" similar to the shine of a cat's eyes on dark nights.

Together these two facts—huge eye with light-reflecting layer—lead to an inescapable conclusion: The horse is a nocturnal animal! To anyone who has studied zebras in the wild this will come as no great surprise, for herds of zebras are intensely active in very dim light at dawn and dusk and can obviously see much better than human beings in those conditions. But we are so used to thinking of the domestic horse as a daytime steed that we have overlooked this important aspect of its natural life-style. Riders who have risked jumping with their horses on moonlit nights report that, although it may be a nerve-racking experience for the human involved, the equine partner takes it all literally in his stride.

The fact that the horse is naturally active by night does

not mean that it is naturally inactive by day. It is even more active by day and is in fact both strongly diurnal *and* nocturnal. Throughout the long waking phases of the day and night, the horse's eye is forever scanning the horizon on the lookout for possible killers. And the eye is beautifully designed to be supersensitive to tiny movements in the distance. Even today, after living its whole life in a completely lion-free world, a domestic horse can still be panicked by the sudden fluttering of a sheet of paper in the wind, somewhere at the edge of its range of vision. The old fears die hard.

Helping it in this vigil is its huge range of vision. A horse can see about 340 of the 360 degrees around it, with only two small blind spots, just in front and immediately behind its body. For this reason it is crucial not to approach a horse, even a normally docile one, from those angles. Its sudden realization that someone has come close to it, when an invisible hand pats or strokes it, may startle it badly. Always approach a horse from slightly to one side, where it can see you clearly.

Because the eyes of the horse are set on either side of its head, it does not normally see objects in depth, with binocular vision. It sees them flat, as we do if we shut one eye. It also sees less detail than we do, but is much more sensitive to movement than we are.

Despite this predominantly lateral vision, the horse is capable of a narrow band of three-dimensional vision if it directs its gaze immediately forward. But because of its long muzzle, this vision only works at a distance of more than six feet in front of the animal's head. This is a sobering thought for any jump-jockey because it means that every time he urges his steed into another huge leap over a fence, the animal is jumping blind. As the horse approaches the jump it can see it clearly with both eyes, but then at the last moment the jump disappears from view, blocked by the obstruction of the horse's own head. To use an airport analogy it is as though it is jumping by instruments. It sees the jump coming and then memorizes its position as it sails blindly through the air. This explains why a show-jumping horse sometimes crashes into a fence as if it had not seen it. What happens on such occasions is that something else has momentarily caught the animal's eye and distracted it, leaving it with no defense against the rapidly approaching obstacle. A close study of jumping horses reveals that they frequently try to turn the head slightly at the last moment, to get at least a one-eyed view of the barrier they are scaling. There is no harm in this providing they do not twist the head too soon, in which case they will lose the all-important depth information that will allow them to judge the distance of the jump ahead of them and calculate their leap accordingly.

For many years horses were said to be color blind but we now know that this is not the case, although color vision is much weaker in them than it is in us. They are most responsive to yellows, then greens, then blues, and least of all to reds, according to recent experiments.

In strong light, when a horse is narrowing its pupils, there is a striking difference from the human reaction. In us the circular pupil simply becomes smaller, ending up as a tiny black dot. In horses the pupil narrows to a slit, but not a vertical slit like a cat's. Instead it shrinks to a *horizontal* slit. This is a special adaptation to the horse's need to keep wide horizons in view at all times. The pupils may be smaller in the glare, but the huge range of vision remains unimpaired.

Finally, how far can horses see with clarity? The answer to this question is surprising. In a contest between rival Arab horsemen it was established that a horse could identify its owner from other men at distances of over a quarter of a mile. How they did this remains in doubt, but it was probably identification of characteristic movements rather than details. But in whatever way they managed it, it underlines the fact that the eye of a horse is a truly remarkable organ.

# How Much Do Horses Sleep?

Animals vary greatly in the amount of sleep they need. Cats slumber for sixteen hours a day—twice as much as we do. Horses, on the other hand, sleep for less than three hours in every twenty-four—little more than a third of our normal amount. The difference between the cat and the horse, of course, is that the cat is a predator and the horse is a typical prey species. The horse's wild ancestors were hunted by both daytime and nighttime predators and could afford to spend very few hours in that vulnerable state of deep slumber. Instead they favored long rest periods without actually dozing off.

A careful analysis of some stallions housed in stalls revealed that on average they spent their twenty-four hours as follows: nineteen and a quarter hours alert; two hours drowsy but awake; two hours in light sleep; three quarters of an hour in deep sleep. Not only was there less sleep in general, but the pattern of what there was was also different from ours in that it was broken up into short segments. There were about nine periods of deep sleep, lasting about five minutes for each period. And drowsiness was even more fragmented, the two hours being broken up into an average of thirty-three short snoozes of about three and a half minutes each.

The horse's secret is that, unlike us, it can rest its body remarkably well while standing on all four legs. It does not have our nonstop balancing act to contend with, an act that forces us to lie down for eight hours every night. This is borne out by the fact that horses only lie down for a total of two hours a day. In fact, it is easier for a horse to rest standing than lying down. There is a greater energy demand in a recumbent posture, caused by the pressure of the horse's heavy body against the ground on which it is lying. Blood circulation and respiration are much more difficult in this position. Adult female horses spend even less time lying down than males or juveniles.

# How Do Horses Feed?

This may seem a simple question, but it is surprising how much misunderstanding there is about equine feeding behavior. Hardly any domestic horses are allowed to feed naturally and the results are often unpleasant. To understand what has gone wrong it helps to study the unrestricted feeding actions of rough-living, feral horses.

The first startling fact to emerge is that, given complete freedom, horses spend as much as sixteen hours a day feeding. Intrepid field observers have discovered that they even keep eating in the dark—as late as midnight—and then start up again in the early hours of the morning. The feeding is slow and selective, the horses working away at the vegetation with their amazingly active and mobile lips, sifting and choosing just the plants they want and pushing the others to one side with great dexterity. They seek variety. Although grasses are their main food, they also eat flowers, fruits, berries, and nuts when the mood takes them. If they find themselves near water they gorge on aquatic plants. If the land is bare they will paw the ground digging up roots. If the grass is low they will switch to browsing on leaves. In other words, given free choice, they eat a varied and interesting herbivorous diet.

They eat much more slowly than cattle, for a good

reason. Horses have comparatively small stomachs and unlike cows they have only one stomach. Cows eat for about eight hours a day, munching and swallowing quickly, then spend a total of eight more hours chewing the cud—bringing wads of undigested food back up into their mouths for prolonged grinding. Horses nibble, chew, swallow, and then digest, little by little. They are uncomfortable if their small stomachs are empty, and so they can hardly ever relax.

One mystifying feature of equine feeding is that horses can never vomit. They are simply incapable of it, having special one-way valves that prevent the food in their stomachs being "thrown up." For this reason they have to be especially careful and cautious in selecting their food plants because if they did consume something poisonous they could not cure themselves by being sick. Nobody knows why this shortcoming should exist in horse anatomy, but exist it does and makes feeding a risky business if there are many poisonous plants or other noxious substances in their environment.

Given that the natural feeding behavior of horses involves endless, varied grazing, how does the feeding routine of the stabled horse compare with the free-roaming animal? Badly, is the short answer. In stables, horses are usually given only three feeds a day—rather like people—and the rest of the time they have to stand around and occupy themselves with something else. This does not mean that they are nutritionally underfed. The fodder they are given is concentrated and of high quality. But it does mean that they are behaviorally underfed, and the consequences are well known. The stabled horse fed artificially in this way is liable to develop what are unfairly referred to as "vices."

The most common stable vices are crib-chewing, wind-sucking, lip-smacking, tongue-swallowing, dung-eating, bed-eating, and rug-chewing. All of these are actions that the horses perform to relieve the endless boredom of simply standing still in a sterile little stable, and more specifically to replace the missing grazing actions. It does not make sense to give a horse all the nutrients it needs quickly, since each animal has a genetically programmed "grazing time" of at least twelve hours a day, and preferably sixteen hours, which it wants to fill with feeding activity, regardless of whether it has had the appropriate food intake or not. The horse is essentially a *low*-grade food specialist. It is programmed to spend ages consuming low-grade nutrients with plenty of fiber and bulk. To give horses high-grade food that they can eat rapidly goes against their basic nature. For many of them the outcome is "vacuum eating"—chewing at the crib, nibbling at the wood of the stable doors, swallowing air that distends the stomach and makes it feel full even when it is not, and eating dung that gives at least a little variety to the diet by adding a new flavor.

Fortunately these vices do not occur in the majority of stabled animals, although they can be found somewhere in almost every equine establishment. Somehow most high-grade-fodder horses manage to adapt to their unnatural regime. Their urge to go on and on grazing all day is still there, but it is suppressed. It may show itself in unusual ways—as when a particular horse becomes a "bad-doer" or is "temperamental and high-strung." Many of the problems of stabled horses, although seemingly remote from feeding problems, are in reality traceable back to the artificiality of modern feeding routines. But horses are such amenable creatures and they do their best to adjust to the bizarre human habit of having only three square meals a day. Perhaps it is just as well they do because if they did have free access to food they would put on weight dramatically and begin to develop the silhouette of round-bellied zebras, rather than sleekly elegant steeds. For under natural conditions, horses would face bad periods each year—freezing cold in the northern climates every winter, when even sixteen hours of feeding a day would not result in much actual food intake, and searing drought in the warmer regions, where the feeding would involve many hours of arduous scraping with pawing hooves and resorting to bark-scraping and other emergency actions. To cope with these lean times, wild horses need to be fat—too fat to please a fastidious horseman, and much too fat to satisfy a racehorse trainer. So the feeding problem will remain. It could be eased, however, by a few simple tricks, such as providing low-grade foodstuffs that take a long time for the animal to obtain. Fodder hung in a small-holed net has been suggested as one solution, where the horses must work away hour after hour to obtain small amounts of food. With a little ingenuity in the stable it might be possible to put back some of the natural quality of the feeding behavior and it is a step that might have remarkable effects on the temperaments of the stabled animals.

# How Is Horse Society Organized?

Horses are highly social animals and suffer in solitary confinement just as we do. This fact is ignored by far too many horse owners, who seem to think that their own companionship is sufficient for their animals. More thoughtful horse experts, experimenting with keeping their stallions and mares together, have discovered that natural groupings help to encourage the development of equine "social skills." Their horses become better at coping with stress. They are more relaxed when taken to strange surroundings and generally speaking have more balanced personalities than those that are kept in the more traditional isolated way. Fears of dominance clashes between horses sharing accommodation have proved to be greatly overrated. Friendships between horses appear to be more important to them than matters of status. To understand why this should be, it is necessary to take a look at how bands of wild or feral horses organize themselves socially.

Wild-living horse bands vary in size from two to twenty-one individuals, but the vast majority of them contain between three and seven animals. A typical group consists of a mature stallion, his mares, and their foals. In other words, the horse is by nature a harem species, with the stallion refusing to allow other adult males anywhere near his females. The mares are intensely protective of their young ones during their first year of life, but then, when the next foal arrives the following year, the older offspring soon find themselves in trouble. This is especially true if they are young males. The stallion starts to attack them and drive them away from his band when they are about eighteen months old, and they must retreat to a safe distance and there establish themselves in a small bachelor group. Some of the fillies also leave the band, but the stallion is less aggressive toward them and their departure may simply be the result of the fact that he ignores them and does not try to keep them herded in close to him with the adult mares. The young fillies may wander off and perhaps join up with a bachelor group. Out of this new group a boss male will emerge and, as time passes, a new stallion will be seen to set himself up as harem master, gathering a few more fillies around him and chasing off his male companions.

An alternative strategy for a vigorous young stallion in a bachelor group is eventually to challenge one of the older males with a long-established harem. Attempts at harem takeovers of this kind always lead to serious fighting between the old king and the young pretender. The old king always wins unless he is growing weak, has been injured, or has in some other way become unhealthy. When he reaches this sad condition he may find himself unable to defeat the strong young male and drive him away. Instead he himself must slink off, leaving his familiar group of mares to the control of the new stallion.

The word "leader" has not been used in talking about the dominant stallion, because in reality he is much more likely to be following rather than leading. He may be the boss but he is no tyrant. Instead he is a hardworking group organizer. The decisions about when the band will move off and in which direction it will move are commonly made by the mares. The stallion, seeing them departing, follows to keep an eye on them. He cannot take the risk that they might approach a maturing colt and become too interested in him. Careful studies of wild bands of horses have revealed that whenever one horse was seen to be trailing behind the others as the group moved off, in 73 percent of cases it was the stallion.

Sometimes the decision to take a particular direction is the action of one of the youngsters in the group. The growing foals are full of curiosity and it is only natural for them to dart off eagerly to explore something new. Amusingly, when they do this they often check themselves and wait for a more senior horse to follow after them and overtake them. In this way they are able to initiate a movement without assailing the dignity of their elders, on the principle that seniors will adopt a junior idea just so long as they can be made to think that it is their own.

Although the stallion is content to trail after his band of females and their foals most of the time, he is active in keeping them herded together, rather like an attentive sheepdog. He can allow them to move off as a group but he cannot allow them to scatter. He herds them by running around aggressively, with ears flattened and neck outstretched and waving about. His great moment as a dominant animal arrives when a strange male comes close. Then and only then does he start to act like a harem tyrant, positioning himself between the intruding male and his females, ready for battle. But even then his aggression is all outward to the other male. He seldom shows anything but benign protectiveness toward his mares and young.

The situation changes when there is overcrowding. Stallions are then so likely to meet strange males as the band moves about that each harem master must remain ever on the alert. This requires leading rather than following and in such cases the *leading* horse in the band is the stallion himself in 77 percent of cases—a massive shift from band-follower to band-leader.

The stallion may get help, both from his mares and from his young colts, when driving off intruders, although he rarely needs this assistance. His mares may also drive away strange females that wish to join his harem, and even he himself may repel them—presumably in cases where he already has more than enough females to cope with and cannot tolerate the swelling of his harem group to a size that he would find exhausting to control and service.

It used to be said that within each group of horses there was a rigid "pecking order"—a system of dominance and subordination that meant that each animal knew its exact status in relation to all others at all times. We now know that this is not strictly true. Instead there is a shifting, changing system of dominance relationships, with the context always playing a vital role. One animal may be dominant over another in one social context, but subordinate or equal in another. The reason why there are such complications is that horses are strongly "affiliative." That is to say they develop very tight bonds of affection for one another and when a powerful friendship has been established it can disrupt the usual, simple dominance pecking order and make it much more complex. Careful studies have revealed that mother/offspring, brother/brother, and sister/sister attachments are frequently particularly strong, resulting in special relationships that ignore the usual dispute rules. The result is a society based on friendships and context dominance, rather than rigid formal dominance.

This statement will come as no surprise to those who have kept horses together in groups, rather than isolated in separate stalls. They will have observed that horses housed in groups, in fields or paddocks, will soon start to display all kinds of idiosyncratic preferences for particular com-

panions and distaste for others. These will lead to mild
rivalries for affection and a variety of strange partnerships
and attachments that will only become disputed when
there is too little space, too big a population of horses, or
some special commodity over which a dispute must
inevitably arise. Then and only then will the tight bonds of
equine friendship start to fray and snap. For at heart the
horse is a friendly, cooperative creature among its own
kind, displaying a softness of character that has led all too
easily to the exploitation of the species by mankind. A less
sociable animal would have repelled all boarders and
would have sent would-be riders packing.

# How Do Horses Show Affection
# for One Another?

Like many mammals, horses display their friendship for one another by acts of mutual cleaning. Being groomed by its mother is one of the earliest and most basic rewards for the young foal, second only to being suckled. Having its coat gently nibbled comes to represent moments of peace, security, and maternal love. When the foal matures it retains this association between grooming and affection.

When it is born the foal is carefully licked by the mare for about the first half an hour of its life. Licking then almost vanishes as a mode of grooming and is replaced by delicate biting movements that help to keep the coat in good condition, freeing matted patches, removing loose hair, clearing away dead skin, and opening clogged pores to enhance sweating. When it is a few days old the foal may indulge in reciprocal nibbling with the mare, but at first these bouts are few and far between. The earliest recorded mutual session of this kind was between a three-day-old foal and its mother, but this was exceptional. By the end of the first week of life it starts to occur more often and the frequency increases steadily in the month ahead. The young animal may also be seen in mutual grooming with another foal, the sessions lasting up to several minutes. The peak of this activity is reached between the ages of three and four months.

Having established this mutual aid system in infancy, horses continue to use it throughout their adult lives. In a wild-living adult band, grooming sessions can be used by human observers as indicators of the relationships within the group. The more friendly two horses are, the more they groom one another. Rival horses rarely indulge in this pattern of behavior. It is most likely to be the weaker of the two animals that initiates the bout of grooming, careful studies revealing that it is the subordinate that approaches the dominant one in 62 percent of cases. However, it is the dominant partner that nearly always brings the session to a close.

Each bout starts with the two animals sniffing one another and then, facing in opposite directions, moving closer so that each can nibble the other's mane. This is the most popular area of the body for grooming, accounting for 60 percent of all the nibbles. There are two reasons for this: The mane is the most difficult part of the body for a horse to keep clean itself, and in addition the long hairs there need more attention than the shorter body hairs. From the manes, the nibbling spreads to take in the sides of the neck, the shoulders, and the back, as far as the base of the tail—all areas that are hard to deal with without a little help from a friend. A solitary horse can roll on its back on the ground, or rub up against a branch or a tree trunk, but these are crude, imprecise actions. Only the finely tuned nibbling of the mutual grooming session can deal with specific points of irritation efficiently.

Sometimes, when they have worked their way down one side of the body, the two companions turn around and repeat the process along the opposite side, starting out at the head end again. These double-sided sessions may extend up to thirty minutes, but they are rare. Ninety percent of all grooming bouts last no longer than three minutes. The frequency with which they occur varies from season to season, but they are most common in the spring and summer. The spring peak coincides with the shedding of the winter coat, and the second peak, at the height of summer, is explained by the need for shade. Driven together in quietly resting, shade-hugging groups, wild-living horses are literally thrust under one another's noses, and this encourages extra grooming.

In addition to mutual nibbling, horses that are troubled by insects indulge in mutual tail-swishing. Standing close together on a hot, fly-buzzing day, they repeatedly flick their tails over the faces of their companions. Sometimes whole groups of horses swish away together, clearing the surrounding air of troublesome pests. Detailed studies of wild-living horses have revealed that those living in groups where this action is possible suffer from far fewer horsefly bites than those living separately.

Mutual aid actions are so characteristic of friendly relations that they continue even in cases where the coats are in perfect condition and need no real cleaning. The grooming has become an end in itself, a gesture of "belonging" and a symbol of the bond between the equine companions. Because of this, the grooming of horses by their human owners has a vital significance. It is much more than a simple matter of making the horse look neat and tidy. In the horse's mind, the lengthy grooming sessions it receives are an indication that its human companion is its close friend. For this reason it is always better for the horse's rider also to be its "groomer." This will ensure a tight emotional bond between the two and will mean that the horse always wants to please the rider when they are traveling together. Where the rider and the groom are two different people, the bond of attachment will be weaker between rider and horse.

Apart from the elaborate grooming sessions of expert

horsemen and horsewomen, there is another way in which the natural behavior of equines can be utilized to human advantage. Whenever a human meets a strange horse for the first time, the animal's suspicions and fears can be reduced by performing actions that approximate the start of a horse-to-horse cleaning session. Sniffing the horse's nostrils during the initial approach is the best way of greeting the animal, followed by a "finger-nibbling" of its mane, in which the thumb and bent fingers act as though they were the opposing incisors of a companion horse's nibbling mouth. Working up and down the mane with this finger-nibbling will indicate to a horse that you wish to be friendly and will mean more to it than the pats and slaps that are so often administered. The only drawback to this approach is that it sometimes works so well that the human finds himself or herself receiving nibbles from the horse in reply. Twisting its head around as far as it can, it may return your compliment with such vigorous grooming actions that your clothes never look quite the same again.

# How Do Horses Perform
# Their Courtship?

When the days lengthen in the spring the mares reach their peak sexual condition. Their hormonal systems are activated by the increase in daylight. They can be mated at any time from March to September, coming into heat every three weeks until a stallion has made them pregnant. Each period of heat lasts about five days, with the actual ovulation taking place on the fourth day. There are, however, many minor variations on this pattern with domesticated mares.

The first sign that a mare is coming into heat is that she starts to increase the number of times she urinates. Her urine now contains chemicals that transmit a sexually arousing fragrance and cause the male to perform the strange *flehmen* face in which he curls his upper lip and sniffs the air intensely.

Attracted by the mare in this way he starts to approach her. His own increase in sex hormones has had the effect of enlarging the muscles of his neck and shoulders—the equine equivalent of a macho display. This is emphasized by the way he arches his neck as he comes close to the mare, with his nose tucked in and his tightly curved neck bulging with stallion appeal. He emits long, forceful nickering sounds, raises his tail, and starts to "dance" to his female. The dance consists of a curious, high-stepping prancing action as he circles around the mare. It is caused by a powerful conflict that is going on inside him—a conflict between sexual attraction and fear.

To understand why a mighty stallion should be afraid of his mare it is only necessary to watch what happens when an inexperienced male becomes rashly impatient. As he approaches the female from behind she suddenly stamps her feet, squeals, and kicks out savagely backward. These kicks can seriously damage the health of an imprudent stallion and the more experienced of them learn to watch carefully for signs of female acceptance.

Many mares, when they are only half-ready to mate, become teases. They signal to the male by urinating, high-stepping, standing still, and winking. Then when he closes in excitedly the mare quickly turns, squeals, and lashes out at him. It is little wonder that his courtship is a mixture of intense lust and equally intense fear. When he is certain that the female is prepared to stand still, he approaches more closely. At first he moves in to her neck region and starts to distract her with a little friendly grooming, rubbing, and nuzzling. Cautiously he works his way back along her flanks until he can risk sniffing, licking, and nibbling her rump, tail, and back legs. As a variation he may rub his shoulder against her rump.

The more ready the female is the more she winks at her stallion, but not in a human fashion. She does not wink with her eye but with her vulva, opening it slightly to reveal a brief flash of pink and then closing it again. This excites him further and, if she now stands still with her back braced and with her tail raised to one side, he may risk trying to mount. By this time her lack of aggression toward him will have allowed his fear to subside and made it possible for him to gain an erection. As he mounts her from behind, he has to maneuver his huge, twenty-inch-long penis into the correct position for intromission. He may not achieve this immediately, but once he has done so the act of copulation will be over in a matter of seconds. Authorities differ on precisely how long is involved, possibly because they have looked at different breeds of horses. One gives a time of 12 to 26 seconds, another 14 to 43, and a third 5 to 60. A typical mating act sees the male mount, make seven rapid pelvic thrusts, and then ejaculate 9 to 16 seconds after rising onto the female's back. As he ejaculates, with six to nine spurts, his tail rises and falls in what has been termed tail-flagging. This flagging is a sign to horse owners watching that the female is receiving the male's sperm, and that fertilization will probably soon take place. After about thirty seconds the male dismounts and one minute after mounting his penis is retracted and he wanders off to graze.

In rare cases a female is more interested in mating than is the male, and will approach the stallion and start grooming and licking the sheath, from which the penis emerges when erect. This action sometimes has the desired effect, but such a male may simply be satiated and have no further interest in mounting. A typical stallion has had enough after three copulations in one day. After that, even the most eager mare will have little success with him. One free-ranging stallion of unusual vigor was, however, observed to copulate six times in one day, with three different mares.

If the mating act itself appears to be somewhat abbreviated, it is important to remember that the secret of the wild horse's success has always been its swift escape from danger. Through the whole of the day it must ever be on the alert, always ready for a sudden panic flight. If sexual encounters involved prolonged copulatory connections between male and female—as does occur with many other species, for example, dogs—they would render the horse vulnerable to predators. For a panic species such as the horse even the most intense emotional moments must be as brief as possible. This may explain why the male horse has such a massive penis, the sexual strategy of the species being intense stimulation to produce an almost instantaneous orgasm.

# Do Horses Exhibit Color Prejudice?

This may sound like an extraordinary question. Surely there are no racist horses? Amazingly there are. Certain stallions have been noticed to mate only with mares of a particular color. Other mares are ignored or rejected as sexual companions.

A careful study of free-living feral horses in the United States revealed that different stallions would collect around them different-colored mares when assembling their harems. One stallion preferred buckskin mares, another chose bay mares, and yet another favored very pale-colored mares. The cause of these preferences is not known for certain but it probably relates to the color of the stallion's mother when he was a tiny foal following her shape wherever she went. At this vulnerable stage a male foal may become fixated on his mother's coat color and this fixation may then last into adult life, even where the context has changed to a purely sexual one.

These preferences would be of little more than academic interest were it not for the fact that champion stud males are expected to perform sexually with any high-grade mare they are offered. Yet occasionally they simply refuse to react to a particular mare and the owners are left completely mystified. The solution in such cases is to cover the unappealing female with a large horse blanket, the color of the stallion's mother, prior to mating, or to conceal the mare's true colors in some other way.

The most famous example of this choosiness was one particular champion stud male, the offspring of an English Derby winner, who totally refused to mount any gray mare. The stallion in question, named Little Cloud, would only perform with such females if they were first draped in a rug to conceal their offending whiteness.

Coverups of this kind are not too difficult to manage because, where champion studs are concerned, the unfortunate animals are never allowed the pleasure of free mating. The risk of the male being injured by a kick in the chest is considered too great. So the rewards of being a great champion are not as exciting as most people imagine.

The mares in such cases are given a worthless tease stallion to work them up into a suitably erotic state, so that they will stay quiet and stand for the great one. He is then led in and encouraged to mount her straight away, without any courtship preliminaries. If there is even the slightest alarm that she will strike out, she is fitted with huge soft covers on her rear feet, to soften any blow, or alternatively she is hobbled so that she is completely incapable of resisting the champion's high-priced advances. Where sexual matters are concerned it is much better to be a free-ranging horse living in a natural herd, rather than a pampered—and severely hampered—champion.

# How Does a Mare Deal with
# Her Newborn Foal?

As she comes to the end of her pregnancy, the mare shows signs of restlessness, a clear indication that birth is imminent. This unease is not simply a matter of bodily discomfort—it also reflects a special state of mind. The mare experiences a mood of anxiety, and there is a very good reason for this. She is about to become vulnerable— more vulnerable than she will be at any other time in her life. This may be no great hazard for a much-loved and well-tended domestic horse, but it is her ancient ancestry that speaks to her now, telling her to take care in her impending moment of almost complete helplessness. For a hungry predator in the wild, a mare giving birth to a foal is easy pickings, and precautions are necessary.

The mare has evolved a remarkable mechanism, not clearly understood, by which she is able to control the timing of the birth so that she is alone and in the dark. More than 90 percent of all equine births take place in the middle of the night, and if the mare is part of a natural herd the birth takes place away from the other animals. Intriguingly, the mare will, if possible, seek out some damp or marshy land as a place to drop her foal, as if something about wet ground has a special advantage at this time. In domestic horses living in a field with a pond this has been known to lead to the drowning of the foal, the unfortunate newborn being deposited straight into the water. But in the wild this curious attraction to wet places may well have a more useful role, ensuring that the mare is close to a place where drinking will pose no problems during her vulnerable phase. Alternatively, the marshy areas may offer better cover for the young animal and may simply reflect a search for some kind of natural camouflage.

One consequence of the mare's urge to be alone at birth is that the presence of eager human companions, all too ready to give rarely needed assistance, is very disturbing to her. The mare has a special way of dealing with such intrusions. She waits. She controls her contractions and bides her time. Eventually the nocturnal vigil is relaxed and the watchers retire briefly for a warming drink. No sooner have they departed than she drops the foal. Many horse owners who return to find a new foal tottering to its feet believe that it is simply bad luck that they have missed the great moment, but if they compared notes with other owners they would soon realize that it was not a matter of luck, but of the Garbo-like personality of the foaling mare.

In a natural herd, one birth can quickly trigger off others, suggesting that mares can not only delay their moment of labor, but also advance it slightly. For this reason it is difficult to give an accurate figure for the gestation period of the horse. In one wild-living group it was observed to vary from 336 days up to more than 392. For a mare in a stable gestation usually lasts between 340 and 350 days.

Signs that the mare is near her time include a sudden turning of the head as if to inspect the flank region (checking no doubt the strange feelings emanating from there), pawing the ground, sweating, shifting about, lying down, and then getting up again. Sometimes she may kick against her belly with her hind legs, as if irritated by the growing tension there. At last she lies down and labor begins. The birth sac appears first, like an opaque balloon, and then the increasing contractions of the abdomen burst this fetal membrane and release the fluid in which the unborn foal has been lying. The mare is fascinated by the liquid pouring from her and sniffs it with great concentration, curling back her upper lip in the *flehmen* facial expression. This indicates that she is carefully checking the odor of the fluid, an important part of becoming familiar with her new foal.

Now the front feet of the foal appear and quickly the rest of the young animal follows. The whole birth is usually over in just a few minutes. In the wild, an animal like a horse cannot afford to dwell on this process or rest too long. Any early equines that did so were easy prey and did not live to pass on their genes to later generations.

As soon as the foal has emerged into the world, its eyes wide open, it tries to raise its head. The mare bends her neck around and makes gentle contact with the little animal, nose to nose. As she does so, she gives it a soft vocal greeting—a little nickering noise—and sometimes the foal answers. The bond of attachment is beginning.

When the birth is over, after a while, the mare rises and in so doing breaks the umbilical cord and automatically separates the foal from her body. She then starts licking the young one's mouth and nose, cleaning out the nostrils and aiding respiration. The foal makes mouthing movements as she touches it, the same kind of action that it will use when seeking her nipple. This is the primary action of all newborn animals and it is not long before the foal is feeding greedily. Before this can happen, however, the mare insists on further cleansing and starts to lick and nibble the foal's wet coat, working all over its body. Impatient to rise, the tiny animal keeps trying to heave itself up, only to be pushed back down again in its mother's determined efforts to dry it and, at the same time, to become acutely familiar with its personal body fragrance. Later on this odor will permit her to identify her offspring and distinguish it from other foals, even in the dark.

Two mistakes made by overeager humans attending an equine birth are the cutting of the cord and the rubbing dry of the wet foal. The mare does not get up or pull away from the foal for some time after the birth and until she does so the cord remains attached. There is a reason for this: The foal is getting a last dose of the mare's blood, which will help improve its immunity against infection. Also, time is needed for the natural sealing-off of the blood vessels at the point where the cord joins the belly of the foal. If humans rush in and sever the cord too soon, they can only do damage. Also it is vital for the mare, not the human owners, to clean the foal's wet body, because in this way she becomes emotionally attached to the young animal's scent. Many cases of foals being rejected by their mothers stem from human "helpfulness" that has accidentally weakened the natural bonding process.

The timing of these various stages is as follows. The actual delivery may take anything from a few minutes up to three-quarters of an hour, although it is very rare for it to be lengthy. About 15 minutes after the birth is complete the young animal starts to struggle to raise the front end of its body off the ground. After about 25 minutes it shows binocular vision, and after 40 minutes the ears begin to react by twisting toward specific sounds. When several hundred foals were carefully studied, it was found that the average time for them to stand up on all fours was 57 minutes after birth. Some managed it in only a quarter of an hour, others took over two hours. The average time to reach the point of the very first feed at the mare's nipple was 111 minutes from birth. Again, some foals were precocious, managing this stage in as little as half an hour. Once the young animal has tasted the delights of its mother's milk, it returns time and time again during the hours that follow, the intervals varying from 10 minutes to an hour and a half. Foals have small stomachs and prefer frequent but small meals.

During its early days, the foal keeps close to its mother and she is likely to drive away any curious members of the herd that come too close. She will continue to feed it throughout most of its first year, until her next foal arrives, when she rather suddenly rejects it in favor of the new-comer. The natural age for weaning is therefore between nine and twelve months.

# At What Rate Does the Foal Develop?

Compared with a human infant, the young equine develops at lightning speed. Within a day of its birth it can not only see, hear, nurse, stand, walk, urinate, and defecate, but also follow the mare, vocalize, trot, canter, gallop, play, roll, scratch and groom itself, whisk its tail to remove flies, and even swim.

During the first month of life the foal is intensely inquisitive and playful, exploring the world around it as much as its mother will allow. The mare has to keep a constant eye on her offspring for signs of danger. The milk teeth erupt during this period and the young animal starts nibbling at the ground. In particular it seeks out the droppings of other horses and eats a little of the fresh dung it finds. This apparently aberrant behavior is in reality normal and essential, because it is the foal's way of infecting its own gut with the bacteria vital to its adult digestion. At this phase of its life, the young animal will sleep or rest for about half of each hour. And it will spend about two-thirds of its resting time actually lying down on the grass. By the time it is six months old, this resting time will have been cut to no more than a quarter of each hour, with most of it spent standing up. The six-month-old foal lies down for only about five minutes per hour.

As sleeping decreases, so grazing increases. A four-month-old foal spends roughly a quarter of its daylight hours grazing, but once it has reached twelve months this figure has risen to nearly half. (To be precise, from sixteen to forty-four minutes per hour.)

During this first year of life the young horse becomes a social being. If it is with other horses, it learns that it is a horse by the time it is two months old. But if a young foal is hand-reared by humans from birth until it is two months old and is only then introduced for the first time to other horses, it is terrified of them and retreats to the company of humans for protection. In other words, by the time it is two months old the horse has become irreversibly attached to its "parent" species. To adjust successfully to the dual life of the domestic horse, enjoying the company of both horses and people, a young foal should therefore be exposed as much as possible to *both* species during the first eight weeks of its life.

Between the ages of three months and six months each young horse that is allowed the free company of other foals will go through an important phase of "social play"—play that involves repeated mock-fighting, with rearing, striking, biting, kicking, chasing, and fleeing. These are friendly fights, often interspersed with mutual grooming, and are never savage or vicious. They are much more common in colts than fillies. Colts also exhibit a great deal of juvenile sexual behavior. Even in their first month of life they show (often toward their mothers) attempted mounting behavior, at an average rate of once in five hours.

Occasionally juvenile play is directed at adults. Mares tend to drive foals away if they are not their own offspring, but stallions are surprisingly tolerant. They permit youngsters to attack them and treat their assaults with remarkable restraint, even permitting mane-biting and leg-nibbling, but as the foals begin to mature the stallions' attitude changes. They may tolerate a certain amount of rough play and frolicking from yearlings and even two-year-olds, but three-year-olds are a different matter. By that age, fighting becomes serious and playtime is over. If a young adult male starts to approach a mare in a sexual manner now, he is driven away savagely by the stallion and forced to take up a subordinate position on the outskirts of the herd. The tensions and stresses of the social hierarchy of adult equine life are now upon him.

Although three-year-old horses are fertile, their fertility will continue to increase during the next few years and they can be considered fully sexually mature when they are five. By this age, wild-living males would be attempting to control mares of their own, but would still have to contend with the older and more experienced stallions. With the passage of each year they would become more and more likely to succeed as dominant males, until eventually their strength too started to decline. Stallions can still breed when they are in their twenties, but their fertility starts to wane after they pass through the ten-to-fifteen-year-old period of their lives.

# What Is the Lifespan of
the Horse?

The typical lifespan of a Thoroughbred horse is twenty years. With crossbreds it is slightly longer. It is possible to produce a simple chart showing the approximate relationship between the ages of humans and horses, although this is no more than a rough guide:

| Age of human | Age of horse |
| --- | --- |
| 20 | 5 |
| 40 | 10 |
| 50 | 15 |
| 60 | 20 |
| 70 | 25 |
| 80 | 30 |
| 90 | 35 |

A working horse is reckoned to be old at about seventeen years, its legs usually being the first part of its body to fail. As it gets still older, gray hairs begin to appear on the face, especially around the eyes and muzzle, and there is a deepening of the hollows above the eyes. The eyelids become wrinkled and there is a looseness in the lips, which tend to hang down floppily from the mouth. The back of the animal becomes more and more hollow and the gait when walking much stiffer.

Record lifespans for horses are remarkable, being so far beyond the average. The world record is sixty-two years, for an eighteenth-century horse in England called Old Billy, who was born in 1760 and died in 1822. He was a crossbred, employed to tow barges on the canal near Warrington in Lancashire. He was still working at the age of fifty-nine, if we are to believe the old records, although his workload by then was probably little more than a token. To employ a horse of that age to perform physical tasks is rather like asking a man of 150 to do heavy manual labor. Old Billy was either a most exceptional individual or the records of two Old Billies have been accidentally or deliberately condensed into one, as sometimes used to happen in earlier days.

The oldest pony recorded lived in France to the age of fifty-four years and the oldest Thoroughbred racehorse managed forty-two years (Tango Duke, 1935–78, in Australia). Other exceptional records include another barge horse that lived to sixty-one years, a hunter that managed fifty-two years, and a farm horse that was still working at forty-three. One horse owner had three horses that lived to thirty-nine, thirty-seven, and thirty-five years, revealing that his understanding of horse care went beyond mere luck. But these are all highly unusual cases and nobody should feel they have failed their animals if they do not attain such splendid lifespans. Twenty to twenty-five years is a good life for any horse.

# How Do a Horse's Teeth
# Show Its Age?

The old saying "Never look a gift-horse in the mouth" reflects the fact that it is possible to judge if a horse is old and worn-out by examining its teeth. As the horse grows, so the appearance of its teeth changes and it is easy to estimate its approximate age from the length, shape, and color of its incisors. The following guide may be used:

*At birth*        The newborn foal has only two small incisors in the upper jaw and two in the lower jaw. These are the milk incisors and will be replaced later by the adult teeth.

*At 4–6 weeks*   Two more incisors are added in each jaw. The first, or central, incisors are now flanked by the second, or middle, incisors.

*At 6 months*   Two more incisors are added in each jaw, outside the others. These are the third, or corner, incisors. This now gives the young horse its total number of incisors: twelve (six upper and six lower). These are still the temporary or milk teeth. They all have "cups," that is to say, small concavities at their tips. These little dips will disappear as the teeth are worn down, and this is one of the key factors in determining the age of a horse.

*At 1 year*  The first incisors have lost their cups—they have been worn down to the point where the tips are smooth. The second and third incisors still retain cups.

*At 1½ years*  Now the first and second incisors have both lost their cups and been worn smooth, but the third incisors still show cups.

*At 2 years*  All cups have been worn down and all incisor tips are smooth.

*At 2½ years*  The first incisors of the milk tooth set have been replaced by the larger permanent teeth, with cups.

*At 3½ years*  The second incisors of the milk tooth set have now also been replaced and also display cups.

*At 4½ years*  All milk teeth incisors have now been replaced with larger permanent teeth and all display cups. Technically the horse is now an adult.

*At 7 years*  The first permanent incisors are now smooth from wear, but the others still show cups.

*At 8 years*  The second permanent incisors are now smooth from wear as well, but the third still show cups.

*At 9 years*  All incisors have now worn smooth. All cups have gone. On the first and second incisors there is a new feature: the dental star. This is a short dark line between where the cup used to be and the front edge of the tooth. It is the upper end of the pulp cavity, revealed externally by the wear on the tip of the tooth. Dental stars first started to show at six years of age but inconspicuously and only on the first incisors. They are now clearly visible on both first and second.

*At 10 years*    The dental star is now visible on all incisors.

*At 13 years*    The ends of the teeth become rounder in section and the dental star becomes a centralized dark spot.

*At 15 years*    The outer side of the third upper incisors shows a conspicuous longitudinal groove from the gum-line down the tooth to about halfway from its tip. This dark groove began when the horse was only ten but was then barely visible.

*At 20 years*    The groove on the third upper incisor now extends for the whole length of the tooth.

*At 25 years*    The groove has disappeared from the upper part of the tooth and is visible only in the lower half.

*At 30 years*    The groove has disappeared completely.

From this chart it is clear that at each age there is some telltale clue by which we can assess the approximate age of the horse. Crooked horse dealers are upset by this dental display and try to trick their customers by filing the teeth of older horses to make them look like youngsters. This is a process known as "Bishoping," after a man called Bishop who invented the idea of excavating smooth-tipped teeth with a sharp instrument to recreate the missing "cup" or dip. The freshly excavated surface in the new, artificial cup was then aged by coloring it with the application of a hot iron. The old horse's feelings concerning this brutal method of rejuvenation are not recorded.

While on the subject of teeth, the total number in the skull of an adult horse is forty. Just behind the twelve incisors there are four small canines. Then there is a gap—the space in which the horse's bit will sit when it is being driven or ridden—and beyond it are twenty-four molars or grinding cheek teeth. The front twelve of these cheek teeth (three on each side of each jaw) are represented as milk teeth and replaced at the same time as the incisor milk teeth, but the back twelve do not appear until later, their first arrival being as adult, permanent teeth.

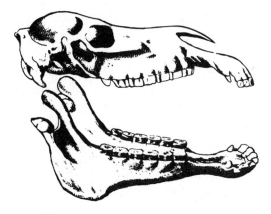

# How Intelligent Is the Horse?

There is an old saying that horses must be intelligent because they never place bets on people. But just how bright are they? One famous horseman expressed the opinion that they "can't have much in the upper story, or they would never allow humans to sit on their backs for more than a split second." Certainly their legendary cooperativeness toward their two-legged companions makes them appear unwise, since it has caused them nothing but trouble over the centuries. But that willingness to tolerate our exploitation of them is really only part of their natural herd behavior. They are such social animals and so responsive to the dictates of the tyrants of their own species that there is nothing particularly surprising about their readiness to subordinate themselves to forceful human beings. This aspect of their behavior does not rule out the possibility that they may be extremely intelligent animals.

Intelligence is the degree to which we can use old experiences to solve new problems. It requires good sense organs to provide information about the environment; good memory to store this information in a retrievable form; and a complex brain to cross-refer the separate memories when searching for an answer to some new challenge.

The problem with all questions of animal intelligence is

finding some objective method of measuring it. Each species has its own way of showing how clever it is, and it is important to devise appropriate tests for each species before drawing conclusions. If we judge a species by intelligence tests that would suit *us* we will almost certainly be missing the point.

In the wild, prey and predator species differ slightly in their "styles" of intelligence. If a predator makes a mistake and its prey escapes, it can live to prowl again. But if prey animals such as horses make a mistake, it can mean sudden death, and for this reason they are particularly sensitive to experiences in which they suffer pain or fear. One nasty moment in a particular place or with a particular individual and a horse may react violently the next time the situation is encountered. If the pain or panic is intense, the animals may commit the experience to memory for years. This can give rise to some seemingly inexplicable behavior. A mature horse suddenly rears up and bolts when confronted with a piece of apparatus or a special location. The new owner cannot understand what is going on. A normally docile animal is suddenly a nervous wreck. Many errors are made in attempting to interpret such behavior, when in fact the hidden explanation is usually that, as a tiny foal perhaps, the horse suffered one bad experience and has been harboring it ever since. This may make horses look stupid, but in equine terms the opposite is the case. They are simply being judiciously cautious, and we should never refer to the timidity of horses as suggesting lack of intelligence. Rather it is the intelligence of a prey species.

Another difference between us and them that is crucial when discussing horse intelligence is the presence or absence of hands. We express so many of our learning skills through our fingers and the way we literally manipulate the world around us that it is hard for us to conceive the world through the mind of an animal with blunt hooves. Inside its brain a horse may well have worked out how to solve a particular problem, but then simply lacks the hands with which to implement the solution. Sometimes the teeth and muscular lips can come to the rescue, however, and when they do they reveal to us the complex workings of the equine brain. For example, individual horses have often discovered how to open the doors of their stalls or stables and escape, or gain the company of their companions. Some find out how to lift latches, others how to remove a horizontal bar. Still others develop ways of improving their meals. One animal decided it hated dry fodder and took to pushing its hay nearer and nearer to its water bowl. It then picked up mouthfuls of dry hay and dunked them in the water bowl before eating them. In this way it used its intelligence to re-create something closer to fresh grass, its favorite food. This was not a rigid or accidental piece of behavior. If fresh grass itself was given, or if the dry hay was dunked before being offered to the horse, the fodder was never dunked before being eaten. If the water bowl was substituted with buckets of water, the dunking was shifted to these buckets. The behavior was flexible and always aimed at the same goal—to avoid boringly dry fodder.

Tests to analyze the discrimination abilities of horses have produced some remarkable results. Given pairs of patterns to look at, such as a square versus a circle, a circle versus a semicircle, or a triangle versus some dots, with a food reward only given for one of each of these pairs, horses learned very quickly to react to the correct one. When twenty pairs of patterns were offered, horses learned to tell them apart in every case (compared with thirteen in donkeys and ten in zebras). Their scores were always well above the 50 percent level of chance and in some cases were 100 percent correct. Their lowest score was as high as 73 percent, with one difficult pair. Even more impressive was the fact that twelve months after the training session there was virtually no memory loss with nineteen out of the twenty pairs of patterns. This is better than most humans could manage and reflects the fact that in the wild it is vitally important for horses to learn and memorize many different plants in their environment—those that taste good, those that sting or prick, those that are distasteful, and those that are poisonous. It is also essential that the learning is retained for a very long period of time—long enough for the appropriate reaction still to be there when the annual cycle of plant growth repeats itself.

The sensitivity of a horse's powers to discriminate between tiny environmental cues is well illustrated by the famous "counting horse" called Clever Hans. This animal was supposed to be able to make a series of simple calculations and to give the answers by tapping his foot. What is $2 \times 3$? The horse would be asked this question by his trainer and would then tap his foot six times. The watching crowd was amazed. How did he do it? At first investigators believed that the animal's trainer must be giving clues to the horse, so they asked him to withdraw. The horse *still* managed to get the right answers. So what was the secret? The next step was to remove the watching audience and put the horse behind screens. This did stop him getting the answers correct and revealed what was taking place, namely that Clever Hans was able to pick up tiny changes in posture or expression as he approached the correct number of taps. All members of the audience knew what the right answer was and apparently tensed up as the foot-tapping reached that point. The horse sensing them, as it were, holding their breath in case he made a mistake, stopped tapping and appeared to have calculated the solution to the mathematical problem. If he could not see them, he simply went on and on tapping. This occurred even when people knew how it was done. Human beings appear to be almost incapable of preventing themselves from revealing their mood by their body language (unless they are professional poker players) and the horse is so incredibly sensitive to slight changes in muscle tone or body posture that it can detect even the smallest unconscious change.

Given this degree of sensitivity, it is strange that competitive horses on the racetrack, or in the show-jumping arena, are not more devious in their treatment of their distinguished riders. A racehorse must soon learn that if it is near the front at the end of a race, it is likely to be whipped all through the final furlong, to drive it on for a prize. If it is hopelessly behind and has no chance of winning it should also discover that it will simply be allowed to tail off and will never be whipped. Since many successful horses win time and again and are repeatedly whipped for their pains, one can only conclude that the fastest racehorses are not the brightest brains of the equine world. Similarly, the best show-jumpers must soon learn that if they manage a clear round they will be asked to do it all again, whereas if they tip over half the fences or shy away from certain of the more fearsome-looking jumps, they will not be asked to prolong the ordeal. Only a stupid horse or one that actually enjoys the jumping ritual would be prepared to do well.

Perhaps, after all, the top jumping horses are less concerned about the severity of some of the jumps than the caring humans who watch their brave struggles. Certainly few horses are as completely helpless in dealing with their riders as some people seem to imagine. It is easy enough for them to learn what is demanded of them and then stubbornly refuse to perform. And with novice riders they may employ that most intelligent and devious of ploys: the sudden gallop under a low-hanging branch—a maneuver that has often been known to make a lasting impact on an unloved owner.

# How Do Horses Find
# Their Way Home?

In earlier days, before the advent of the motorcar, many a country gentleman would set off on his horse for an evening at the local inn, confident in the knowledge that if at the end of a long session of heavy drinking he was incapable of guiding his steed home, it would find its way there of its own accord. In this respect the drunk rider had a great advantage over the drunk driver.

The question arises as to how the horse knows its way. Over short distances it can easily employ its spatial memory, as we do. In addition, it may well use a mental map of smells. The remembered sequence of twists and turns, the shifting pattern of local odors and fragrances, and, in addition, the passing visual images and familiar sounds all combine to provide more than adequate information. But there are many examples of horses finding their way home over unknown, unfamiliar terrain where ordinary environmental clues are totally useless. How did they manage in those cases?

To quote just two examples: A yearling colt was taken from its mare and transported five miles to territory it had never visited before. After a while it was released and managed to find its way back to the mare in five days. This could, of course, be a lucky accident, but such cases are commonplace and it seems that some special sensory modality is operating to assist the animals. A second example concerns wild horses that are rounded up annually in Virginia. Some are sold at auction and the remainder are released. To regain their homelands they have to cross water and travel a considerable distance and yet within a short space of time they are all back in their original home ranges, with their original, distinct herds re-formed. Again, some special sense must be operating.

We have no proof of what this is in the case of horses, but studies with homing birds have proved conclusively that they are sensitive to shifts in the earth's magnetic fields. Experiments using artificial magnetic fields reveal that it is easy to disrupt the homing ability by changing the magnetic forces operating on the birds. There is every likelihood that most forms of life enjoy this sensory ability and that it is somehow based on the presence of tiny iron particles in the tissues of animals, which operate, in effect, like tiny magnets. It seems almost certain that horses are employing this same method.

An intriguing sideline to this is the poor performance of horses taken to new homes in earthquake zones, such as California. When they first arrive, the horses often seem deeply disturbed by the almost ever-present seismological upheavals. These are often too small to be detected by human beings, but they result in alterations in the local magnetic fields, which no doubt give the horses a sense of unease when they first encounter them—rather like country dwellers moving to a noisy city and finding it stressful after the peace of rural life. After a while, the horses adjust to the situation, damp down their responses, and improve their performance, but their initial distress does appear to reveal a marked sensitivity to magnetic conditions, supporting the idea that magnetic factors may be involved in equine homing.

# How Territorial Are Horses?

Some animals wander over a home range without ever defending their space. Others are strictly territorial, living on a clearly defined area that they defend against intruders. The horse does not fit easily into either of these categories. Sometimes bands of wandering horses show no defensive behavior at all, content to roam an extensive home range without ever attempting to drive off other horses. They may even be prepared to share watering places and grazing zones without any disputes disrupting the peace. All that happens when two small herds meet is that they avoid one another and quietly go their own ways. This is what happens when there is plenty of room for all. Without the pressure of crowding, the territorial imperative is not called into action.

When conditions are slightly more restrictive, then true territorial defense can be observed. If a band of horses meets another under such circumstances then a battle may ensue between the rival leaders, usually the dominant stallions. When this happens, the stallion that "owns" the territory invariably wins and drives off the intruder. A victory in such a case does not lead to prolonged persecution of the beaten stallion—all the winner wants is to repel the enemy, not to destroy him—and once he has withdrawn, peace returns immediately.

For domestic horses kept in stables, the question of territoriality is almost irrelevant. Their world has become so condensed that all sense of home range or defended region is outside their experience. However, a pattern of behavior called "walking the fence" can be observed whenever a stabled horse is allowed out into a new paddock. If the paddock is unfamiliar to it, its immediate response to being released there is to set off on a "territorial patrol" in which, by moving all around the perimeter, it learns the shape and scope of its new space. After this patrolling has been fully expressed, the horse then settles down to a quieter enjoyment of the area it has been allotted.

Even large paddocks are, however, mere miniatures of a natural territory. Wild equines, for example, have been observed to have a range of thirty to eighty square miles. In traveling between grazing, drinking, and sleeping locations, they will cover as much as sixteen miles a day, walking in single file and often keeping to well-worn paths that they know intimately. So for their domesticated cousins there is always going to be a lifetime of greatly reduced circumstances as far as spatial freedom is concerned. Some domestic horses react to this by giving up all hope of behaving territorially. Their world is so cramped, compared with the wild state, that they simply switch off their territorial feelings and accept the smaller, softer life. Others resist this quiet option and may occasionally become fiercely defensive in their small paddocks. Care always has to be taken when a new horse is added to a paddock where another has been for some time. The "owner" may suddenly unleash its pent-up territorial aggression and lash out savagely at the newcomer. Without adequate supervision such an attack may become serious. The established inhabitant, either because it is harboring a grudge over the way it has been treated in the past, or because it feels a desperate need for a bigger territory and cannot accept an intruder on what it considers to be the central core of its world, refuses to be satisfied with the submission of its enemy and continues to attack the victim despite its repeated attempts at appeasement. Unrestrained violence of this sort reflects the abnormal spatial conditions that most domesticated horses must endure in their proximity to man, but fortunately, when it does occur, it can usually be controlled efficiently before any serious damage is done. Only in instances where horses are being kept by novices who fail to recognize that the social world of equines involves serious competition as well as cooperation will there be major risks. Old hands will know from experience that no matter how docile a horse may have become in its relations with its rider it still remains a complex social being once it is turned out with others of its own kind.

# How Do Horses Fight?

Like all intelligent animals, horses attempt to settle their disputes without actually coming to blows. They rely as much as possible on threat displays. With these signals they can usually decide which is going to be the dominant member of a group of equines.

In one intensive field study it was found that only 24 percent of disputes went beyond visual and vocal threats and mild body pushes. This figure was based on no fewer than 1,162 separate disagreements at a water hole. Another, quite separate investigation that looked at the way horses argued over food revealed that the corresponding figure there was 22.6 percent—remarkably close. It is safe to say, then, that three-quarters of all horse disputes are settled without resorting to violence.

The threats given include the following: The ears are laid back, the head is lowered, the neck is extended, the rear end of the body is moved closer to the enemy, the body is used to block the path of the enemy, and the enemy is pushed with the head, neck, shoulder, or body of the attacker.

As the argument becomes more heated, the horse starts to shake and nod its head, the lowered, extended neck making vigorous sideways and up-and-down movements, as though the animal were tearing at the enemy's body in a savage bite. While this is going on the mouth is open, giving a bite threat, but it does not make contact with the enemy's body. The tail starts to swish angrily. The front legs make threat strikes in the direction of the opponent, or they may be stamped on the ground. Or the hind legs may kick out with a threat that unless the enemy retreats it will be given a serious contact kick, rather than one in midair. Head bumps and body bumps may be given and, although these are certainly contact actions, they are not done in such a way that they become fully physical acts of aggression. Loud squeals of rage are often emitted as an embellishment of these threatening actions.

If all this fails, then the horse must finally give in to brute force. To administer this it rears up on its hind legs and strikes downward with its front feet, squealing and biting at the enemy's neck at the same time. Or it may charge at the adversary, neck thrust forward, and attempt to bite it as savagely as possible. These actions—striking and biting— are the signs that the horse in question is a truly dominant individual. If instead it is rather defensive and nervous at the same time as being angry, then a different kind of reaction is observed. Such a horse employs a defensive, as opposed to offensive, assault. The body is swung around rapidly to present the rear end to the opponent. At the same moment the hind legs lash out in what can be a seriously damaging one- or two-legged kick.

Once the fighting has started there is a great deal of mutual rearing-up, and the violent contact may last for several minutes before one individual submits to the other. Submission is signaled simply by the loser turning away and retreating. If it is not able to do this it may offer some specific submissive displays, including the snapping action related to mutual grooming, the head toss in which the head is jerked upward and to one side, the eye stare in which the eyes bulge more than usual, and the tucking in of the tail against the now slightly crouched rear end. Most attackers will respect this degree of appeasement and will break off their attacks. This has sometimes been given as an example of "altruism" in animals, but in reality it is simply the aggressor's way of reducing any chance of an injury to itself. Fighting frequently damages both the vanquished *and* the victor, which is the main reason why it is avoided so assiduously.

# How Fast Can Horses Run?

Horses galloping flat out regularly reach speeds in excess of 30 miles an hour, and if they are healthy Thoroughbreds can maintain such speeds for several miles. Quarterhorses, which, as their name suggests, only race over short distances of a quarter of a mile, have been known to exceed 40 miles an hour. The record over this distance is 43 miles an hour, but that was exceptional. The record at 3 miles is 34 miles an hour.

The longest horse race in history appears to have been over 1,200 miles, in Portugal. The winner was an Egyptian-bred Arab horse called Emir. Another long-distance runner with remarkable stamina was a horse called Champion Crabbet, who traveled 300 miles in 52 hours.

In the early days of steeplechasing, races were sometimes run across country over distances of 8, 12, and even 20 miles, but in modern times these severe tests have largely disappeared, the $4\frac{1}{2}$ miles of the Grand National now being the longest course any top-quality horse is asked to cover. The record for this testing race is 9 minutes, 1.9 seconds, set by the amazing Red Rum in 1973, giving him a speed—over some of the most demanding jumps in the world—of 29 miles an hour.

# What Is the Difference Between Hotbloods and Coldbloods?

There is a tradition with horse breeders that sees all domesticated horses as hotbloods, warmbloods, or cold-bloods. These three types have nothing to do with body temperatures, but with the breeding and origins of the various kinds of horses.

There are only two kinds of hotbloods: the Arabs and the Thoroughbreds. These are the fine-boned aristocrats of the equine world and are sometimes referred to as fullbloods. The name hotblood is associated with them not only because the original stock came from the hot deserts of the Middle East and North Africa but also because they are high-spirited and quick to react.

The coldbloods, by contrast, are the work horses, mostly massive animals with a stolid, calm, placid character. They are heavy-boned, even-tempered, and are descended from the northern forest type of horse—from the tundra horse and the steppe horse. They are not coldblooded, but they do come from the colder, more northerly climes, and their stockier build suits them to the intense cold of the northern winters.

The warmbloods, sometimes called halfbreds in contrast with Thoroughbreds, are crosses between the two extreme types. They are usually fine-boned animals, a characteristic they inherit from their hotblood Arab ancestors, but they are less fiery in temperament and less high-strung. Nevertheless they are much more spirited and quick to react than their coldblood ancestors. These warmbloods are the modern sports horses, developed for all kinds of leisure activities.

# How Many Horse Breeds
# Are There?

A recent survey of horse breeds gives a total of 207 distinct examples. However, some of these may not be valid—many countries and districts have their own local names for "breeds" that are no more than minor variations of better known forms—and there may be many more breeds that are lurking in some remote region, unrecorded. But this figure gives a rough idea of just how richly varied the world of horses is today.

Of these 207 listed breeds, 67 are ponies, 36 are working horses, and 104 are sports horses. In this context, the definition of a pony is any horse that is less than 58 inches (14.2 hands) high, but height is not the only feature that distinguishes ponies from horses. Ponies are much closer to the primeval ancestors of the horse, with shorter legs in relation to the size of the body and with a sturdier build, being weight-for-weight stronger than horses. There are two breeds of small animals that, although technically ponies because of their size, are more horselike in proportion. They are the ancient Caspian breed and the modern Falabella. Both of these are usually referred to as "miniature horses" rather than ponies, to emphasize their more graceful, delicate body proportions. The Caspians, recently rediscovered on the shores of the Caspian Sea in northern Iran, look like tiny Arab horses, and it is believed that they may indeed be close to the original equine from which the Arab horses were developed thousands of years ago. They were depicted in ancient Persian carvings dating from 2,500 years ago but had not been seen by outsiders for at least 1,000 years. Remaining isolated in a small area they continued to breed true and were not tampered with, leaving them much as they were in the ancient world. Then in 1965 some were brought out to the West where they have been carefully bred and protected, a living reminder of what the forerunners of our modern Thoroughbreds looked like.

The Falabella is a very different story, being a modern Argentinian breed that is essentially a much reduced Shetland pony, but with the difference that it has the slender proportions of a tiny horse. The smallest of all living horses, these diminutive animals are far too lightweight to ride and are kept purely as exotic pets. With an average height of less than 34 inches they are considerably smaller than many breeds of dogs. The tiniest adult Falabella stood only 15 inches at the shoulder, compared with 40 inches for the tallest Great Dane. The idea of a horse being able to walk underneath a dog is bizarre, but these minute equines should not be looked upon as freaks, because the ancestor of all modern horses, *Eohippus* the Dawn Horse, which lived fifty million years ago, was only 10 inches high. Today, when Falabella foals are born measuring less than 12 inches at the shoulder, we are looking at something the size of those remote ancestors.

Moving from the ponies to the working horses, we go to the other extreme. These are the giants of the horse world. Some are known to have stood at over 7 feet at the shoulder

(21.1 hands) and have weighed over a ton. These were the heavy horses that gave us agricultural power in the days before the internal combustion engine started to spew its fumes onto our roads and our countryside. Today they survive as cherished relics of those quieter days, magnificent specimens appearing regularly on special occasions at country shows and fairs. Devoted enthusiasts are keeping most of the major breeds alive and interest in them is, if anything, now on the increase, so that their future even in the space age is assured.

By far the most varied group of equines today is, however, the one comprising the hundred breeds of sporting horses. Sport, whether riding, hunting, racing, show-jumping, eventing, or polo, keeps the twentieth-century horse in a permanent position of prominence. As the vast urban populations of cities spread and the countryside is hemmed in more and more, rural pursuits become more fiercely defended and horsemanship perversely—in the era of the automobile and the traffic jam—is flourishing. As an antidote to the mechanization of life it appeals not only to the equestrians themselves but also to the millions who watch them—at racetracks and show-grounds and on television. The sports horse has become more than the object of the enthusiasm and passion of devoted riders—it has become a symbol of man's intimate relationship with animals and of the green past of our rural existence. In this capacity, we may well expect to see even more breeds in the future, rather than fewer.

It is of interest to examine which countries boast the greatest variety of breeds. Russia leads the way with at least twenty-seven; Britain comes second with nineteen; France third with eighteen and the United States and Germany next with sixteen each. Italy has ten and Poland nine. But these are minimum figures, because new breeds are being developed all the time to meet the demands of our changing environment. Nevertheless they are a guide as to which countries have been most active in creating specific breeds of horses and cherishing them right through to the late twentieth century.

# Why Do Horses Run Races?

This may seem a stupid question, but it is not. It is unnatural for horses to gallop at high speed over long distances. So why do they do it? We know why greyhounds race—it is to pursue the hare—but what is it that makes Thoroughbreds run so fast and so far?

To understand the behavior of modern racehorses it is necessary to examine more closely their curious life-style. People who only set eyes on them at the racetrack often have no idea of what a strange, spartan existence they lead. When they are not racing they spend much of their time penned up in their separate stalls. There they become frustrated. Their regular training runs do little to relieve this frustration, serving only to whet the appetite for freedom of movement.

If a novice owner innocently suggests that a racehorse might enjoy being turned out into a field, the trainer will explain that this might take the animal's mind off racing. On this basis horses race because they have been boxed up to such an extent that they have been starved of any kind of powerful physical activity and have an overload of energy just waiting to erupt. On the race day, given their head, they take off at full tilt and run and run until they are exhausted. If this exhaustion sets in before the finish line has been passed they are either whipped or pulled up, according to how good their chances are of winning.

Such is the explosion of muscular activity in a typical horse race that Thoroughbreds are usually not capable of racing again for days. This underlines how unnatural the pattern of their lives has become. No wild horse could survive if it was only capable of rapid fleeing every few days. But then, no wild horse would be expected to flee so far. The natural predators of wild horses—the wild dogs, wolves, and big cats—would kill or give up after a much shorter chase. In effect, when our racehorses rush off eagerly along the open spaces of the racetrack they are behaving rather like schoolchildren, cooped up all day in an unnaturally immobile condition and then let out into the playground for high-intensity activity. Just as much of the play in the playground is mindless and meaningless, so is the racing along the course by the horses. It is not so much that they are fleeing, or reliving a panic escape, but rather that they are expressing themselves physically after a long period of restraint.

Yet, despite this, there is an element of fear and panic-fleeing inherent in the horse race. This element is under-lined by two facts. First, no wild horse would ever accelerate to a full gallop without being in a state of panic-fleeing. Moderate fleeing is done at the trot, when a band of horses is retreating from something suspicious. Only when the predator has broken cover and is in hot pursuit will a wild horse break into a top-speed gallop. So somewhere in a racehorse's mind there must be a fantasy, at least, of a pursuing killer. Second, there is the pain of the whip. As it stings the flank or rump it must be reminiscent of the scratch of a feline claw or the nip of a canine mouth. Feeling this close-proximity attack, the horse makes an extra effort to escape, and continues to do so as long as it has any strength left in its limbs.

Finally, then, racing is a combination of fleeing from invisible predators and the more basic expression of highly thwarted physical activity. It is a kind of "vacuum" or "overflow" activity in which vigorous, healthy young animals seek escape, not from wolves or lions but from the enforced action poverty of their highly artificial lives.

# Why Do Some Horses Run Faster Than Others?

When the horseplayers stare at the horses parading in the paddock before a race they are earnestly seeking some small visual clues as to which will be the fastest runner. Unfortunately the most important part of the horse is not visible to them, for it is its heart that will make the difference between winning and losing. All modern racing horses have superb limbs and muscles and are capable of reaching high speeds. That is not where the real difference lies between one highly bred horse and another. The secret is internal and invisible—for it is ultimately the efficiency of the blood system of each individual Thoroughbred that will be the deciding factor between glory and ignominy.

With each race, the first quarter of a mile is run anaerobically, that is to say, with the animal consuming fuel that does not require oxygen from the blood stream. After that the horse becomes involved in aerobics and it is up to the heart and lungs to supply the necessary oxygen to the muscles. The slightest weakness in the heart or infection in the lungs and the animal will lose its race. So when the racing enthusiast declares that a great racehorse is "all heart," his emotional metaphor has a factual basis.

The most amazing aspect of the physiology of racing is

the tremendous increase in heartbeat speed, from resting to full gallop. Some authorities claim that there is an amazing tenfold increase, from 25 to 250 beats per minute. Others suggest a more modest 36 to 240, but even this means an increase of nearly seven times to a pounding heart level of 4 beats every second. Little wonder that Thoroughbreds look so exhausted after a tough race.

Exertion like this at regular intervals is clearly not a natural phenomenon for equines, but expensive horses running valuable races are asked to do more and more and to do it more and more often. The likely result is an enlarged heart and serious health risks. What happens is that as the heart grows in size it allows no room for "the expansion of effort" during the tension of a demanding race. It has to press harder against the surrounding tissues to do its normal work. This extra pressure tires the heart and the horse "fades" as the race nears its end. Any horseplayer who has bet regularly on "sure things" will know this phenomenon all too well. The horse does splendidly through the early and middle stages of the race, but then suddenly appears to be moving backward. The other horses seem to be streaking past it and accelerating to the finish line. In reality they are all slowing down slightly as they near the limits of their physical abilities, but the horse with an inefficient heart will slow down much more dramatically, creating the false impression that the others are speeding up. If a fading horse is not rested following such a race it may suffer irreversible damage to its heart.

Another important aspect of race winners is their gait. The symmetry with which their legs touch the ground during their galloping movements is of great significance. The ideal horse, it is said, should have legs that operate "like the spokes of a wheel," each one making contact and taking the weight of the horse in its turn to an equal degree and for an equal time interval.

If a horse with a strong heart, a powerful chest, and a symmetrical gait fails to win races then what is wrong with it? Genetics and breeding may be partly to blame, but less than most people imagine. It is generally felt that if you mate two champions you will obtain champion foals, but many pundits have paid huge prices for such foals only to be bitterly disappointed. The truth is that modern Thoroughbreds are so inbred that they all possess very similar genetic constitutions and the offspring of almost any of them could turn out to be champion animals. There is some bias in favor of foals from winners, but it is only that—a bias, not a certainty.

The individual personality of the horse is significant, but it is hard to say how much of this is genetically controlled and how much is the result of the quirks of personal history. The reason we are still in the dark is because racehorses are too precious and too slow-breeding for behavior students to be able to carry out tests on their individual psychology. However, some tests carried out with animals that are easier to handle, such as white mice, have proved that it is possible to "create" winners by simple training methods. Small mice allowed to dominate big, tough mice (by doping the big mice to make them unusually docile for a while) soon began to believe in themselves. When pitted against big mice again (undoped this time) they won their fights with them and became the dominant animals despite their small size. This kind of training technique shows how easy it is to build confidence in any animal, simply by manipulating the way in which it performs in its social encounters. The personal history of every animal is full of little incidents of this kind, and we often do not realize how, in a fleeting moment, a young foal may acquire a feeling of personal strength and determination.

If we knew that the personality of young Thoroughbreds could be "helped" as they mature, we might be able to enhance their stubborn resolve to go on and on running even when the exertion has started to cause them the sort of physical discomfort that human athletes know so well. To understand this determination a little better it is worth looking at the way in which a wild herd of horses flees from trouble. The safest place to be if you are an escaping ungulate, whether a horse, a deer, or an antelope, is in the middle of the herd as it runs away from danger. It is the stragglers that get picked off by predators, and sometimes the front-runners, too. The front-runners, if they go too far ahead of the herd, become just as isolated as the stragglers bringing up the rear, and then they too fall prey to lurking killers—the ones waiting in ambush. So the natural urge of a galloping horse must be to keep with the group; in other words, there is safety in numbers. Translate this into racing terms and you have the typical race winner. If you run films of races backward you see the way in which, nearly always, the winner lies in "midfield" until the last stretch of the race. Frequently it is in third or fourth place, a good position from which to make the last bid for the front. Up to that point, it has felt safe and would probably stay there if it were not for the urging of its jockey. But with the finish line coming close, he drives it on, frequently using the whip to simulate the stinging lash of a predator's claws raking the fleeing animal's rump. This extra stimulus makes the horse surge forward and it passes its companions to win. At the point where it throws caution to the wind and takes up the "front-runner position" its natural fear of getting too far in front of the herd, and thereby becoming a potential victim for predators hiding in ambush, is overcome by the "certainty" that there is a killer slashing at its rear end.

Needless to say, rival jockeys are also whipping their horses at this point, if there is a chance of them winning. So the last furlong is a test of stamina, as each competing horse struggles to escape the "attack" from the rear. And stamina, at the end of a long race, comes back to the question of heart—both literally in terms of blood circulation, and metaphorically in terms of individual personality.

Some champion horses do not need this last-ditch encouragement. They take the lead not so much because they abandon the security of the group but simply because the group is starting to lag behind. They have good "race rhythm," in that they do not race ahead too soon and have to be held back—which wastes precious energy—and they do not lag behind early on and have to be driven hard far too soon. Either way the uneven pace would inevitably consume extra energy. The perfect rhythm is one in which the animal always keeps up steadily with the main body of horses until the final phase when, in racing parlance, the jockey can "press the button" if he needs to and the horse, at his urging, will surge forward with a powerful final run.

# Why Do Some Horses Run Slower Than Others?

After every race a little ritual is performed between the owner, trainer, and jockey of each of the losing horses. This is the "Why we were beaten" ceremony and involves the search for an excuse that will persuade the owner to pay next month's training bills instead of selling off his disappointing horse.

The simple truth is taboo during this ritual. The most obvious comments may not be uttered: that the horse is no good; that the other horses were better; that the jockey rode badly; or that the trainer failed to prepare the horse. It is also forbidden to mention the fact that horses are not machines but living beings susceptible to occasional inconsistencies in their behavior. The astronomical cost of keeping a modern racehorse in training is such that the animal is required to be nothing short of a consistent winner . . . without some very good and very particular reason. This is where the inventiveness of the trainer and jockey are called into play. The same excuse will not do after each lost race. New reasons have to be found.

When one exasperated owner wrote to a sports editor on this topic, giving some of the bizarre excuses he had been offered over the years, the editor was soon flooded with additional examples from other frustrated owners. Here is a modified and simplified selection of them with some additional ones collected personally. The top fifty are:

1. The horse swallowed its tongue.
2. The horse stepped in a rabbit hole on the far side of the track.
3. The horse was hit by a flying piece of turf.
4. The horse swallowed a flying piece of turf.
5. The horse disliked the tight turns.
6. The horse was stung by an insect at the start.
7. The horse was distracted by a television van.
8. The horse did not like the rain.
9. The horse had an abscess in its mouth.
10. The horse had a sore foot.
11. The horse did not want to go past the racetrack stables.
12. The horse suffered from muscle spasms.
13. The horse did not like the high winds.
14. The horse was lazy/was too eager.
15. The horse was bumped during the race.
16. The horse was kicked during the race.
17. The horse disliked the slow pace/disliked the fast pace.
18. The horse jumped too carefully/overjumped.
19. The horse felt crowded in the large field of runners.
20. The horse missed the competition in the very small field of runners.
21. The horse did not act on the hard going/did not act on the soft going.
22. The horse hated the left-handed track/hated the right-handed track.
23. The horse was underworked/was overworked.
24. The horse would improve over a shorter distance/needs a longer trip.

25. The horse missed the start and then had too much to do.
26. The horse was struck in the face by a rival jockey's whip.
27. The horse's saddle was slipping/was too tight and was pinching.
28. The horse was too inexperienced/was too experienced.
29. The horse bolted on the way to the post/bolted at the start.
30. The horse was hemmed in and could not find a gap.
31. The horse traveled badly during the long journey to the racetrack.
32. The horse suffered from exhaust fumes inside the horse trailer.
33. The horse had been upset by a fireworks display near the stables the night before.
34. The horse's girth strap broke.
35. The horse lost a shoe.
36. The horse had come into season.
37. The horse hit the front too soon/needs to be a front-runner.
38. The horse was off its feed.
39. The horse needed the run-out.
40. The horse should not be whipped/needs stronger handling.
41. The horse needs castrating.
42. The horse may have a low blood count.
43. The horse's champion sire did not reach peak form until he was much older.
44. The jockey thought there was another lap/thought there wasn't another lap.
45. The jockey mistakenly thought something was wrong and pulled the horse up.
46. The jockey dropped his whip.
47. The jockey mistook the last furlong post for the finish line and eased off.

48. The jockey was kicked during the race.
49. The handicapper had been too severe and the horse was carrying too much weight.
50. The stable has a virus.


Any racehorse owner who has not been confronted with one of these excuses after a race must possess a miracle horse.

Perhaps the most spectacular excuse for a horse doing badly in a race was that offered by an apprentice jockey who had been hauled up before the stewards to explain his appalling ride. Asked why he had not done better he replied, "Because the gov'nor told me in no circumstances was I to finish in the first six."

# Why Do Racehorses Not Run Faster Each Year?

With each new season human athletes seem to run faster, breaking records in almost every event. On the human racetrack hardly any record is more than a few years old. With Thoroughbred racehorses the scene is very different. Despite careful breeding plans and the investment of huge sums of money, the modern racehorse appears to have come to the end of its line, in terms of speed. Records are broken only rarely and in general there has been little improvement over the past century. Why should this be? Why is it that generation after generation of selective breeding, always favoring the fastest horses, has not led to gradual improvement? Something is clearly amiss.

Racing is an ancient sport. In its earliest form, the horses were not ridden. Rival desert chieftains kept their horses thirsty and then released them at a set distance from a watering place. The first animal to reach the water and drink was the winner. The earliest detailed records of a racehorse trainer date from 3,338 years ago in the Middle East. A little later, in ancient Greece, the first mounted horse races were begun 2,636 years ago. The horses were ridden bareback. About 150 years later special races for mares and for young apprentice riders were introduced. The Romans became racing fanatics and 1,900 years ago there were as many as a hundred races a day. Heavy gambling, vast crowds of spectators, riots, race fixing, bribery, horse doping, and all the other traditional elements of the horse race scene were already much in evidence. But this was not to last. With the fall of the Roman Empire organized horse-racing vanished. The supply of fast oriental horses dried up and the heavier warhorses and working horses came to dominate the scene.

A thousand years passed and then the Middle East exerted its equine influence once more. Crusaders marveled at the swift horses of their enemies and could not resist bringing some back with them when they returned to their European homes. About eight hundred years ago there were weekly races in London, using these speedy imported animals, and the first recorded racing purse was offered to the winner of one such race. The prize was forty gold pounds, a huge sum in those days. But racing did not gain a strong foothold. It remained a minor diversion, with hunting horses and warhorses considered far more important. Only when fast cavalry replaced the heavy horses of the armored knights did equine speed reassert itself as a significant preoccupation. As the centuries passed racing became more and more organized until the stage was set for the birth of modern Thoroughbred racing.

With royal patronage in the eighteenth century serious racing began and the Middle East yet again injected an important element into the English equine scene. Three founding fathers—magnificent Arab stallions—were imported and bred with about fifty mares to start the new line called Thoroughbred. At the end of the century, in 1793 to be precise, the General Stud Book was started, recording the pedigree of each Thoroughbred racehorse. The idea for this was probably borrowed from Arab horse breeders who had been pursuing pure-line breeding for many years and

*111*

who kept records of the ancestry of each of their champion horses. The name Thoroughbred is, in fact, a literal translation of the Arab word *kehilan,* which refers to a horse that has been "pure-bred all through."

Not long after it was started, the Stud Book was closed, that is to say, no new founding stock was permitted to enter it. As a result of this action the next two hundred years of Thoroughbred horse breeding was founded on a very narrow genetic basis. It has recently been estimated that 81 percent of the genetic makeup of all modern Thoroughbreds is based on just thirty-one original horses. To begin with there was room for genetic improvement, with the first hundred years of racing showing almost annual increases in speed. It has been calculated that there was an improvement of about 2 percent per annum until roughly 1900. During the nineteenth century there had been a gradual enlargement of the horses—about 1 inch every twenty-five years—until an average of around 5 feet 4 inches (16 hands) had been reached. The legs had in the process become longer and rangier. The modern racing machine had been perfected. But then it seemed as though the limit had been reached. Many of today's records are half a century old. The great English classic race, the Derby, for example, was run in record time back in 1926, the horse in question managing 38 miles an hour over the $1\frac{1}{2}$ miles. Shorter races were covered in 44 miles an hour. These speeds have not been exceeded, despite the fact that each year there is a greater and greater concentration on breeding from winner after winner and we should expect to see a continuing gradual improvement. This means that either the original genetic "pool" was too narrow, too restricted by the small number of initial founding stock, or that there is something wrong with our present-day training techniques with top racehorses.

If the genetic explanation is correct, then it is time for the sacred Stud Book to be opened once more and for the Middle East influence to be once again injected into our racing bloodstock. If the training technique explanation is correct then we need to look much more closely at the highly artificial life-style of the modern Thoroughbred. If the answer is to "leave matters alone" and to stop meddling in the hallowed traditions of the turf, then it has to be pointed out that racehorses are showing a poor return for the amount of effort that is going into their development. Something is not right and it is time that the racing world risked innovation—either with breeding or training. The problem is that innovation is frightening when potential champion foals are born, and trainers and owners are loath to take risks. So much is at stake. But sooner or later someone will take the plunge and then we will see horse-racing move forward into an even more exciting phase in the twenty-first century.

# Why Do Jockeys Whip
# Their Horses?

Whips are used to steer horses and to make them accelerate. Occasionally and unforgivably they are used to punish them. Many modern critics of horse-racing view all whipping as cruel and unnecessary and there have been strident demands for the total banning of whips in all races. In certain countries the authorities have already placed severe restrictions on the way the whip may be used. In Scandinavia, for example, it is forbidden to remove the whip hand from the reins, thus greatly restricting the action of whipping. Elsewhere the number of times a horse may be struck during a race has been limited. Stewards are always on the lookout for "excessive use of the whip" and overenthusiastic jockeys are punished for their crimes.

Among the voices raised against the whip are some from inside the racing world itself. One great authority on the Thoroughbred horse stated bluntly that, in his opinion, whipping stems from "the inherent tendency in mankind, especially in the lower stages of civilization, to beat unmercifully domestic animals." An ex-trainer exclaimed recently, "The Brutal Billies have had the whip hand long enough." He went on to admit that from his experienced position inside the racing world he was finding himself "increasingly nau-seated by the sight of tired jumpers being flogged." Having made these remarks, he immediately denied that he was growing soft, revealing that he knew all too well the kind of reaction his comment would provoke from the tougher el-ements of the racing world. But even the most ardent horse beaters are beginning to take notice of public opinion. The ex-trainer whose shout "Curse these damn whips!" became a newspaper headline made the telling request that people should "watch those little flat-race jockeys surreptitiously trying to smooth down the welts on their horses' quarters before they come in to unsaddle." In other words, it is not only the authorities but also the whippers themselves who are becoming uneasy about the more sensitive attitude of the general public, a public that increasingly rejects all the old excuses for cruelty to animals.

So what is the final answer? Should the whips go? Many professionals would argue that this would be disastrous, robbing them of a control device that enables them to direct the horse through a crowded field and avoid unnec-essary bumping and barging. They would also argue that a light touch of the whip in the final yards is vital to persuade the horse to leave the security of the pack and stride out in front. If they are right, what is the solution?

A compromise is clearly possible, one in which penalties for harsh whipping are increased. The accusation "ex-cessive use of the whip" must be applied more liberally. The fact is that a light flick of the whip is no more cruel than slapping your own thigh, and with an animal as sensitive as the horse it does the job just as well as the infliction of pain.

If the solution is this easy, why then is there a problem? The answer lies in the enormous pressures that are put upon jockeys to win important races. If the owners of their mounts see them lose a race by a short distance without lashing at their horses' rumps, they are liable to accuse them of not trying hard enough. Gamblers at risk of losing large sums of money can be heard bellowing "Hit him, hit him!" as their chosen horse comes thundering in a close second. It is not that these are particularly cruel men, but the racing fever that possesses them in the final seconds of a race drives them beyond their normal restraints. And this is precisely what happens to some jockeys. They feel that if only they could encourage the horse a little more it could find that extra speed and race past its opponents to finish first. So instead of flicking the whip, they start lashing the horse as hard as they can, trying to drive it on. It is this that certain sections of the public have come to hate and that turns them against the world of horse-racing.

Severe whipping of this kind is far less successful in speeding up a racehorse than these lashing jockeys imagine. Although a touch on the rump gives the horse the idea that there may be a killer striking out at it from behind, and can make it speed up, a really savage blow there can do something else. It can make the horse swerve away from the source of pain. Since the whip always lands on one side or the other of the horse's body this can mean a sudden sideways lurch that can disrupt the animal's rhythm and actually slow it down for a vital split second. So there is no excuse for violent whipping under any circumstances.

# Does a Horse Know When It Has Won a Race?

Despite the sentimentality of the riding world where winning horses are concerned, the answer must be no, it does not know. This is obvious enough when the details of horse-racing are examined, and yet the suggestion that horses are unaware that they have just won large sums of money for their owners, trainers, and jockeys seems to be totally unacceptable to equestrian experts.

During the last stages of any race, a Thoroughbred is straining every muscle, not to win but to please its rider. Horses are highly sensitive and extremely cooperative animals. They come to respect their riders and to be responsive to their every command. A horse knows when the person on its back is urging it on a little faster or slowing it up. It can sense this through the tactile signals it obtains from the direct contact of rider on horse—the touch of the hands, the grip of the legs, the stiffness of the body. If its jockey is pleased it may know this from the way he slaps the side of its neck or cries out with joy. But it cannot possibly connect this pleasure with that all-important act of crossing the finish line just before the other horses. This is a completely human concept and has no meaning whatever to horses.

It is amazing that the equine world finds this so difficult to accept. Yet they themselves frequently do not know who has won a race. When the "Photo Finish" sign goes up at the end of a closely run race, even the humans standing right on the finish line do not know who has won. So what hope does the horse have? Furthermore, in races where there may be as much as a length between first and second, it means nothing to the horse that at the precise moment when it passes a particular white post the outcome of the race is being judged. Indeed, it is doubtful whether the horses understand that they are in a race at all, let alone whether they are winners. All they know is that, after being kept in a small stable, they are allowed out on to a wonderful track along which they are encouraged to move as fast as they can, until they can move no more or until the riders on their backs have relaxed and stop urging them on. To them it is simply an exercise combined with something resembling a herd panic. Competitive racing is not part of their mental outlook and no amount of romantic imagining on the part of equestrians will make it so.

One Irish horse that had just won an important race was greeted by the television commentator's words, "There is one horse that certainly knows he has won a race!" At the time he was saying this the heaving animal, covered in sweat, was surrounded by a gleeful crowd of happy Irish horseplayers who were all slapping the horse joyfully on the neck, flanks, back, rump, and anywhere else they could reach in their moment of explosive pleasure. What the horse was supposed to conclude from this barrage of slaps and shouts is anyone's guess, but one thing is certain: It was not aware that it had just passed a white post a fraction of a second in front of another horse. It may have concluded that it had somehow done something terribly wrong and was being mobbed for it, while other horses were being allowed the luxury of a little peace and quiet, but beyond that it can only have been puzzled and distressed by the clamor and the pressing crowd. Horses may be highly responsive and intelligent animals but they are not human and they are not gamblers. Nor are they geniuses and they certainly never ever know that they have won a race.

# Why Do We Speak of Steeplechasing?

We owe steeplechasing to the cunning of the fox and the dishonesty of humans. The fox enters the story one afternoon in the middle of the eighteenth century when a frustrated group of fox hunters were returning home from a disappointing day's sport. Their chase had been fruitless and not a single fox had been caught. To salvage something from the occasion one of the hunters is said to have issued a challenge on the spur of the moment, wagering that he could reach the clearly visible steeple of the home village first. The object of the race was to make straight for it, regardless of what obstacles were in the way, and touch it with the whip to be declared the winner. Thus was born the jump-racing that to this day we call by its original eighteenth-century name, steeplechasing.

Before this event occurred there had been a long tradition of both flat-racing and hunting, but for some reason nobody had been inventive enough to combine the two. Now they were put together and the new sport quickly gained support. The first recorded steeplechase took place in Ireland in 1752 when a Mr. O'Callaghan and a Mr. Blake raced over $4\frac{1}{2}$ miles starting at Buttevant Church and ending at St. Leger Church. It is recorded that the prize was "a hogshead of claret, a pipe of port, and a quarter-cask of Jamaica rum." It is not, however, recorded who won the contest. Presumably after enjoying the prize no one was in a fit state to record anything.

Dishonest humans enter the story a little later, in 1810 to be precise. Throughout the second half of the eighteenth century steeplechasing, from church to church (or point-to-point, as the saying went), continued to flourish in an informal way, but then at the start of the nineteenth century progressed to the status of a more serious, organized sport. The reason had to do with skulduggery among flat racers. Certain flat races were for hunting horses—horses that were genuinely ridden on the hunting field and were not specifically bred for racing. Some riders pretended that their mounts were hunters when in reality they were speedy Thoroughbreds. They entered them in hunter races and easily beat the heavier, slower jumping horses developed for the tougher pursuit of cross-country running and leaping. To defeat these Thoroughbreds someone suggested adapting for the formal racetrack the crude steeplechasing that was taking place across natural countryside.

The first true steeplechase took place at Bedford over a 3-mile course on which eight fences had been built. The obstacles were made severe enough to defeat any flat-racing horse inexperienced at cross-country jumping. They were $4\frac{1}{2}$ feet high with a strong bar across the top. The novelty of this new type of racing, with the promise of witnessing the proud riders crashing to the ground, attracted a huge crowd of over forty thousand spectators. Ever since then the danger to the riders has added a gruesome appeal to the great jump races. The danger to the horses has caused an equal amount of concern and criticism of these events. The unique Grand National race, first run in 1839 at Aintree, has always drawn vast crowds of enthusiasts but at the same time has been the subject of repeated accusations of animal cruelty. Some owners have refused to allow their much-loved racehorses to be entered for this punishing $4\frac{1}{2}$-mile race and a recent winning owner admitted that she was too horrified to watch her horse gain the great prize. After the race she announced that the horse would never be raced in the National again.

Steeplechasing is most popular—for traditional reasons—in its country of origin. In the United States flat-racing continues to dominate because gamblers are said to avoid the supposedly high-risk jump races, in which even a strong favorite can easily have a nasty accident. Curiously, statistics reveal that their fears are unfounded, because favorites are more likely to win jump races than flat races. But the prejudice remains and steeplechasing has never gained the worldwide popularity of the older flat-racing.

# Who Invented the Stirrups?

It comes as something of a shock to discover that none of the horsemen of ancient Greece or Rome ever used the stirrups. If they went into battle on horseback they did so gripping their mounts with their thighs and hoping for the best. Neither Alexander the Great nor Julius Caesar enjoyed the stability that stirrups give to the rider and this makes it all the more amazing that Alexander and his cavalry were able to conquer vast regions totaling two million square miles. The method used by the early Greek horsemen is revealed by the writings of Xenophon, who advises that the rider must stand "upright with his legs somewhat apart; for thus he will cling more firmly to the horse with his thighs, and, keeping himself erect, he will be able to throw a javelin . . . with greater force."

This thigh-gripping technique, with no saddle and no stirrups, meant that ancient horsemen had to be amazingly fit and immensely expert to stay on their mounts during battle. It restricted their actions considerably and also made quick mounting and dismounting much more difficult. It is hard to understand why, among all the many thousands of early classical horsemen, there was not just one inventive spirit who improvised with some kind of leather saddle and foothold extension. Perhaps it was the rigidity of military training that prevented it and forced the ancient Greeks and Romans to conquer the known world in prolonged discomfort.

So who did invent the stirrups? Russian experts believe it was the Scythians, who lived to the north of the Greeks and who were brilliant horsemen. Early artifacts seem to show horses with stirrups attached to them, but it is hard to be certain. And because Alexander obtained horses from them it seems highly unlikely that he would not have exploited their discovery. We must look elsewhere.

Farther to the east, in a hotter climate where riders went barefooted, there appeared around 200 B.C. a looped rope through which horsemen pushed a big toe as an aid in mounting. This toe stirrup was invented in ancient India and it is to this civilization that we apparently owe this simple but momentous invention. As knowledge of it spread out across Asia, its use extended into the colder regions where horsemen wore heavy boots to keep their feet warm. This footwear necessitated the enlargement of the toe stirrup into a full foot stirrup. In this new, improved form the stirrup gave the riders balance and stability and made it possible for the first time for mounted warriors to use both hands at once for their weapons. Previously, when throwing javelins or spears, the thigh-gripping riders had been forced to cling to their horses' manes with the nonthrowing hand to steady themselves. Now they could fire arrows on the move and perform other much more devastating attacks on their hapless enemies. Armed with this great advantage, the Mongolian hordes under Attila the Hun swept westward, slaying countless victims from the vantage point of their nimble horses. One military historian declared that the stirrup was "the most significant development of warfare between the taming of the horse and the invention of gunpowder."

By the eighth century A.D. the stirrup had come into use

right across Europe and western horsemanship was never the same again. In conjunction with the improved saddle, it gave every rider the chance to feel secure on his steed, to wear heavy suits of protective armor with relative safety, and to mount his horse with ease even if as a rider he was overweight or elderly. Riding was no longer a pursuit solely for young athletes. It could now be practiced by an individual of any age and condition, with both hands freed for any action that might be necessary.

The origin of the stirrup as a loop of rope for mounting is borne out by the origin of the name itself. The word stirrup comes from two ancient words, *stige* and *rap,* meaning literally mount rope or climb rope. Further support comes from the fact that the toe stirrup is still used today at certain southern Indian racetracks, reflecting the well-established tradition that exists in that part of the world for this particular type of horse equipment.

# Why Do Horseshoes Bring Good Luck?

Imitation horseshoes can be found all over the world—on charm bracelets, key rings, wedding cake decorations, greeting cards, and motor vehicles of all kinds. In country districts real ones are also still to be seen, nailed over doors, on outside walls of buildings, and especially over the entrances to stables. Sailors sometimes fix one to the mast of their ship, as Nelson did on the *Victory,* and British taxi drivers even have their own horseshoe superstition, which takes the form of trying to secure a vehicle registration number with a U in it, the U acting as a symbolic horseshoe.

In all these cases the horseshoe has the same significance—it protects and brings good luck. But why should this be? Most people have no idea and simply accept the horseshoe as an emblem of good fortune without questioning its origin. Those who have tried to trace it back to its roots have come up with conflicting ideas. The simplest suggestion sees the protective qualities of the shoe as no more than an echo of the protection that the object gave to the horse's foot on which it was worn. If it prevented the harshness of the earth from damaging the horse, perhaps it can also prevent a hostile world from harming us.

Supporting this idea is the seemingly magical property of the shoe. Why magical? Because when it is fitted to the horse's hoof, hot from the fire, and nailed in position, it causes the animal no pain. This particularly impressed the more superstitious observers who witnessed the shoeing of horses in earlier centuries, at a time when the anatomy of the horse's foot was less well understood.

Helping to make it more magical was the frequent use of seven nails, this being a lucky number. Of the greatest importance was the fact that the shoe was made of iron—a magical substance that was believed to keep the Devil at bay. From the earliest days of ironworking, this metal was considered to be capable of repelling evil spirits, and for many people the phrase "touch iron" for luck was preferred to "touch wood."

This may explain why an iron object was fixed over the door, but why a horseshoe rather than something else? The answer to this lies in its shape. If it is fixed with its arms pointing upward, like a U, it resembles a pair of horns and the use of horns to protect buildings has been known for thousands of years. Originally these horns were symbolic of those sprouting from the head of the ancient Horned God. This was the pagan god that was to become converted into the Devil in later years by devout Christians keen to take over earlier images and defile them. But although the Devil became the enemy, his horns have persisted as a protective device right up until the present. In the form of a finger gesture, the "horned hand" is still used as a lucky charm or performed as a protective sign, and pairs of real horns are fixed high up on many buildings—especially farm buildings—in the Mediterranean region.

Christians, always on the lookout for possible symbol takeovers, did their best to depaganize the lucky horseshoes. They suggested that the shoes should be nailed to the walls on their sides, so that the U-shape became a C-shape. Attached in this way, the C could stand for Christ and it was explained to the gullible that this was the true origin, thus making the old ritual safe for Christianity.

Others preferred to nail the shoe upside down, so that it looked like an inverted U. In this position it was said to be particularly defensive. In some countries a clear distinction was made between the U-shaped shoe (which was primarily concerned with bringing good luck) and the inverted U (which was primarily concerned with protecting). The symbolic significance of the inverted U is said to be that it imitates the shape of the female genitals. If this seems an unlikely subject with which to adorn the outside walls of a house, it should be remembered that many medieval churches displayed clear images of female genitals above their doors. These infamous figures, known as *sheela-na-gigs,* were thought to function as "distractions" to divert the evil spirits that might otherwise have entered the interiors of the buildings and caused havoc there. The inverted-U horseshoe, being less explicit, acted as a more acceptable, euphemistic substitute.

That it did carry a specifically sexual meaning is borne out by the fact that in the eighteenth century the word *horseshoe* was a slang expression for the female genitals, and in Germany there was a saying that if a girl had been seduced she had "lost a horseshoe" (*Sie hat ein Hufeisen verloren*).

More innocently, there are those who see the symbolism of the horseshoe as a sign of sanctity, the curved shape representing a halo. Hung over the house, this halo gives the dwelling sacred protection. Finally, there is the theory that its shape relates to the crescent moon and invokes the protection of the celestial Moon Goddess.

Whichever of these factors has played the bigger role in

giving us the lucky horseshoe of modern times, it is clear that, with a number of symbolic strands working together to support it, it was destined to be a popular and persistent talisman. It is not surprising that it is still being used by millions every year, despite their lack of understanding concerning its origins.

# What Is the Origin of
# Horse-Brasses?

Today we think of horse-brasses as purely decorative—attractive adornments that we add to the trappings of heavy horses on gala occasions. In reality, however, they have a much more significant role in the history of horses, being a last remnant of ancient, pagan beliefs. For horse-brasses are, in origin, protective amulets to defend the horse against evil spirits. As such they can be traced back thousands of years, almost to the beginning of man's involvement with the horse.

As soon as horses came under human control they gave their owners such an enormous advantage over their horseless companions, followers, or rivals that each trained horse became a precious, revered object. To superstitious minds this meant that it would automatically attract the attention of the powers of darkness—powers that would stop at nothing to harm and destroy such a magnificent possession. They were thought to employ a special device through which they inflicted their havoc—namely the Evil Eye. So cunning were these malevolent forces that it was impossible to tell who might be possessed of the Evil Eye. Any stranger looking at your wonderful steed might strike it down with a single glance, causing it some mysterious illness, injury, or death. Anyone with a squint or an odd-colored eye was highly suspect, but you could never be certain, because the individual through which the dark powers operated might not be aware of what was happening.

In this fear-ridden world of supernatural beliefs, pagan religions employed all kinds of safeguards, from sacred rites and solemn rituals to blood sacrifices and hideous penances. One comparatively harmless element among all this mumbo jumbo was the wearing of protective ornaments called talismans or amulets. These had some property about them that either repelled the Evil Eye, making it look away before it could do any harm, or fascinated it so much that its interest was deflected. It could be repelled by powerful symbols of Good, to counteract its Evil. And it could be deflected by offering it obscene images that appealed to its base nature. Horse-brasses favored the first of these two strategies. They repelled the Evil Eye by using images of the powerful pagan gods—horns, the sun, and the crescent moon.

It is these images that are central to the design of horse-brasses and it is amusing to think of the devoutly Christian Victorian horse owner busily polishing up his symbols of ancient sun worship and moon worship, and paying his unwitting homage to the ancient horned god. It was always believed that the Evil Eye would be at its most active at those times when the potential victim was triumphant—on special celebratory occasions—so it became particularly important to deck the horses with protective symbols at all great festivals and grand events. It is this that we are witnessing today when, in a spectacular parade, show, or fair, the heavy horses are displayed wearing their ornate trappings festooned with glittering horse-brasses. Nobody may be aware of what this is really about, not even the horse owners themselves. Superficially, it has become no more than an appealingly decorative event, but beneath the surface it is a pagan spectacle.

Looking at the individual designs, it is clear that the simple, plain sun disk is the primary form and this is still used today in pride of place on the horse's forehead, where it is known as the "Sunflash." It is called this because it flashes gold in the sun as the animal moves. This is an important quality of all horse-brasses, and the reason why they were polished so ardently in earlier times is that by glittering in the sun they were thought to dazzle the Evil Eye and in this way repel it even more successfully. Dull trappings were considered to be far less effective.

In addition to the circular sun disk, there was also the rayed sun or sunburst. Other ancient emblems included swastikas (symbols of the sun moving through the heavens), moons, stars, wheels, hearts (borrowed from ancient Egypt), sacred hands, horns, acorns, birds, beasts, and flowers, especially the lotus flower (another Egyptian motif). These were the earliest images, but in Victorian times there was a sudden rush to increase the number of patterns and before long there were literally hundreds to choose from, although the designs of the new ones owed little to their pagan roots. Now, almost anything that took the Victorians' fancy was included and earlier traditions were gradually forgotten. It has been estimated that there were no fewer than seven hundred different figures portrayed and a thousand abstract patterns. Some authorities put the total as high as three thousand different designs—a challenge for any obsessive collector. Since 1820 the hammered brasses have been replaced by cast ones and in recent times these have been mass-produced, not for horses but for sale directly to enthusiasts without their ever being used. There is an irony in the fact that the amulets intended to protect the draught horse from destruction have outlived it. They were clearly not effective against those staring Evil Eyes of the twentieth century, the headlights of the automobile.

# Why Do We Not Eat Horses?

Horseflesh is highly nutritious and by all accounts tastes good. So why is there such a powerful taboo against eating it? This taboo is not, as some may imagine, a modern development of horse-loving nations, with people becoming increasingly sensitive about eating their animal companions. It has a much more ancient and more obscure origin. Over a thousand years ago, for example, the subject was taken seriously enough for the pope to issue an order totally prohibiting the eating of horseflesh under any circumstances.

To understand how this came about we have to look right back to the very beginning of man's relationship with the horse. We know from the bones found in Ice Age cave dwellings that our early ancestors hunted and ate horses on a large scale. The favored method of obtaining horseflesh then was to make a herd of wild horses panic and fall over the edge of a cliff. This crude technique was refined as the hunting of the Old Stone Age gave way to the farming of the New Stone Age. Now groups of wild horses were rounded up and kept under human control. As domestication progressed, additional uses were found for the horse. Although still mainly kept as a source of meat, it also provided tough hides for clothing and for covering simple shelters, mare's milk for drinking, and bone and hoof for implements and ornaments.

Such exploitation was never taken to extremes, however, as it was with certain other domestic animals such as cattle. There was no equine equivalent of the heavy-bodied beef cattle or the large-uddered milk cattle. The early horses stayed much as they had always been. The reason for this was that, from about five thousand years ago right up to the present day, the horse has had one dominant role in human life—that of a beast of burden, a means of transporting first human belongings and then human beings themselves.

The laden or ridden horse transformed human life in a dramatic way. Hitherto undreamed-of mobility and warfare of a deadly kind were now possible. The horse, in short, was becoming the most important animal known to man. Little wonder that legends were woven around it and that it became increasingly revered and eventually even sacred. For superstitious people it became clear that only such a marvelous animal as the horse was fit for the gods. Only the horse could carry the gods through the skies and this explained the frightening (and, in early days, inexplicable) sounds of thunder and lightning. They were, it was fervently believed, the roar of the heavenly hooves and the crack of the heavenly whip.

Because of its association with powerful deities, the horse inevitably became an important sacrificial animal in many of the earlier pagan religions. Believers gained strength by eating its flesh and drinking its blood. And it is this that is the key to the later taboo on devouring horseflesh. For when Christianity began to spread and gain momentum, it mounted a campaign of new rules, which discredited the sacred customs of the old religions. In this way the devouring of horseflesh became wicked and dirty.

In some areas this reduction of the horse's role from

sacred being to mere beast of burden was difficult to achieve, and horse-eating continued despite the urgings of the Christian church. That is why, in A.D. 732, Pope Gregory III was forced to lay down the papal law on this subject. The Celts, with their special goddess of horses called Epona, were so stubbornly resistant to the new Christian dictum that even as late as the twelfth century an Irish king was required, at his inauguration, to take a bath in horse soup. A white mare was ritually slaughtered, butchered, and boiled to make a broth. The new king then sat in the broth, ate pieces of horseflesh, and literally drank his own bathwater.

Pagan horse-eating persisted here and there for several more centuries but eventually died out almost entirely throughout the Christian world. Other major religions were also opposed to it. Buddha specifically prohibited it. Mohammed never ate horseflesh and, although he never outlawed it, few Moslems today will touch it. The same is true for Hindus.

As a result of these widespread religious restrictions, horse-eating became very rare. It surfaced only as a much maligned practice of the starving and those suffering from extreme poverty. Battlefields strewn with the carcasses of valiant warhorses were too rich in precious protein to be ignored by wartorn peasants. But there was always unease about such scavenging. This unease has lasted right down to the present day, with a blanket of silence being thrown over the disposal of the bodies of dead horses. If they are to be eaten, they are often exported first, to hide the deed, or they are consigned to the anonymity of the pet food trade.

There was one remarkable attempt to revive horse-eating in Europe, but it failed miserably. Surprisingly it came in the middle of the last century at a time when the Victorians were at their most sentimental about animals. It was caused by official concern over the bad diet of the poorer classes. Since many people were suffering from serious malnutrition, the enormous waste of good horseflesh that was common at the time was viewed as unacceptable and serious attempts were made to glamorize this freely available but scorned source of meat. In 1868 a special society was formed in England called the Society for the Propagation of Horse Flesh as an Article of Food. An amazing and much publicized dinner was held at the august Langham Hotel in London. The menu included the following items among its nine courses: horse soup; fillet of sole in horse-oil; terrine of lean horse-liver; fillet of roast Pegasus; turkey with horse-chestnuts; sirloin of horse stuffed with Centaur; braised rump of horse; chicken garnished with horse-talons; gladiator's rissoles; tongue of Trojan horse; lobster in old-hack-oil; and jellied horses' hooves in Maraschino. There was also a buffet of collared horse-head, baron of horse, and boiled withers.

The sober, economic side to this curious propaganda was that widespread epidemics had cut a swathe through the cattle population and beef prices had soared. If horses—then numbered in their millions as a means of transport—could have been exploited at the end of their trotting days, an immensely valuable new meat supply would have become available: if only people could have been weaned onto this new (or, to be more correct, ancient) form of food. But they could not. Pockets of acceptance were established in some countries, especially France and Belgium with their *chevaline* enthusiasts, but in general the attempt was a failure. The magazine *Punch* summed it up by giving two definitions: *hippophagy*—the eating of horseflesh; *hypocrisy*—saying horseflesh is very good.

A Cambridge don, in an attempt to avoid assailing the nobility of the horse, turned his attentions to the more

*137*

humble donkey. He had a nine-year-old animal fattened and butchered for the Master's table at Trinity College, but the idea never caught on. Its failure was aided by Oxford dons who were quick to remark that for the head of a Cambridge college to devour an old donkey was tantamount to cannibalism.

The church, perhaps because it had forgotten all about Celtic horse goddesses and the religious roots of the horseflesh taboo, was silent about these Victorian attempts to reintroduce horsemeat to the human menu. The failure was due instead to a new attitude toward animal life. Darwin had shown that human beings are related to other species and a stronger "fellow-feeling" was growing. With it came animal welfare organizations and widespread opposition to animal cruelty. Vegetarianism was becoming an organized movement for the first time. People were generally less bloodthirsty where animals were concerned. At Holy Communion they still drank the blood of Christ and ate his flesh, in a sanitized Christian adaptation of the earlier pagan feasts where the blood and flesh of sacred horses were consumed, but the blood was now cheap wine and the flesh was no more than thin wafers of biscuit.

The new mood was one in which only animals whose sole purpose on the farm was to provide food were acceptable on the menu. Any other domestic animals were taboo because we had a different kind of contract with them. Horses, dogs, and cats were our servants and our companions and were not for eating. If an old horse had given its life to supporting us on its back, then it deserved some reward at the end of its working life. Homes for retired horses suddenly seemed more appropriate than the glue factory. And so it has remained, with the new sensitivity maintaining the ancient taboo, but for very different reasons.

# What Is Horsepower?

For many years automobiles and other forms of engine were given horsepower values to indicate their strength. It was fondly and not unreasonably believed by most car owners that an 8-horsepower car was as powerful as eight horses. This was not, however, the case.

The idea of using horsepower as a measure of the strength of engines was conceived by the Scottish engineer James Watt as a way of making his newfangled steam engines more understandable. In the eighteenth century people were used to thinking in terms of the work rate of horses and so this provided a familiar grading system for the new machinery.

In order to calculate the power of a horse, Watt went to the London breweries where strong dray horses were toiling and carried out a series of measurements, arriving at a figure that he thought represented a fair average. This was the true horsepower, but for some strange reason he decided to multiply it by 1.5 to produce his official figure for the power of one horse, which was 33,000 foot-pounds per minute (or the power needed to shift 33,000 pounds a distance of one foot in one minute). He did this, it is said, "in order to rate his steam engines conservatively in terms of horsepower." In other words, to be 10 horsepower an engine had to have the power of fifteen muscular dray horses. This curious decision was the opposite of bragging and was presumably intended to make the actual strength of his machines surprising rather than disappointing after mental comparison with a team of horses.

From the very beginning his horsepower system came under attack. It was described as "a new and shockingly unscientific unit . . . insensibly coming into use." Despite this it remained in popular use for many years because people could easily equate the power of their automobiles with the power of a team of horses pulling them along. It gave early automobiles an image of massive strength, which made up for their many faults and drawbacks.

# Why Do We Call Professional Riders Jockeys?

In earlier centuries the name Jack was used as a general term for any unidentified man "of the common people." In Scotland peasants were given the same familiar name, but with the slightly different pronunciation: Jock. The juvenile version of Jock, applied especially to lads working as grooms, was Jockie. By the early seventeenth century this term was widely applied to young horse dealers. These young professional horse handlers provided the original source from which the first hired riders were drawn for racing. By the late seventeenth century the word *jockey* had come into being as the name for any professional rider and has remained with us ever since in this role. So, in origin at least, a jockey is a young Scottish peasant.

This is the generally accepted source of the word, but there is one voice of dissent. A Victorian expert insisted that "The word *jockey* is neither more nor less than the term *chukni* slightly modified, by which the gypsies designate the formidable whips which they usually carry, and which are at present in general use among horse-traffickers under the title of jockey-whips." Other scholars refer to this idea as mere fancy and dismiss it out of hand, but it may well have played a secondary role in fixing the name.

It has certainly remained well fixed, for it has spread to many other languages including French, Spanish, Portuguese, and German.

Incidentally, the familiar jockey's cap was borrowed from an ancient Roman design developed for charioteers. They wore a bronze version that protected their skulls from damage and that bore a peak that shielded their eyes from the often dazzling sun. The same design was borrowed for English schoolboys' caps.

# Why Is a Horse Called a Horse?

Most of us use names like "horse," "pony," "stallion," "mare," and "foal" without ever considering where they came from. They are simply part of the language and we leave it at that. But if we look closer at their origins some intriguing facts come to light.

### Horse

Experts still argue about the origin of this word, but the favorite theory is that in ancient times a similar term meant "swift" or "running" and that our modern name has grown out of that. This seems reasonable enough when it is recalled that increased mobility for human horse owners was the primary advantage in the domestication of this species.

### Pony

Today we use the name *pony* for a small horse that is not more than 58 inches (14.2 hands) high, regardless of age or sex, but it has not always meant this. It started out as the Latin word *pullus,* meaning a foal. From this developed the word *pullanus,* meaning a colt. In Old French this became transformed into *poulain,* and a small colt was given the special title of *poulenet.* When it reached Scotland, this word (pronounced "pool-ney") was modified to *powney* (pronounced "poo-ney") by dropping the "l." There it became strongly associated with the tiny Scottish horses found in the Shetlands and elsewhere. About two hundred years ago, dictionaries referred to ponies as "little Scotch horses," so it seems that we owe our modern term to the Scots, "poo-ney" becoming "po-ny" in pronunciation as it traveled back south of the border.

### Stallion

An adult male horse that has not been castrated has been called a stallion since the fourteenth century. It means literally "one kept in a stall"—the "stall-i-on"—and it was applied to an entire male horse because such an animal was housed in a separate compartment, or stall, due to its boisterous nature. The term appears to have originated in Italy, where there was an early word *stallione* from which our modern name has descended.

### Mare

This is an Anglo-Saxon name in origin. The Anglo-Saxon word for horses in general was *mearh* and the feminine of this was *mere,* from which we obtained the modern mare for an adult female horse.

### Foal

From the time of its birth until it has been weaned any young horse is known as a foal. This comes from its Anglo-Saxon name, *fola.* The corresponding feminine is *filly,* and we still use this term today for any young female horse, from the time it is weaned until it is four years old.

## Colt

The name *colt,* which today signifies a weaned male horse until it is four years old, has not always had this narrow meaning. For example, it is found in the seventeenth-century translation of the book of Genesis, where there is a reference to "thirty camels with their colts." Another Biblical mention describes a colt as "the foal of an ass." Clearly the term was not originally intended to refer specifically to young male equines, but to young animals of a much more general kind. Also, it was at first applied to both sexes, and one could speak of a "female colt." But as time passed it became confined more and more to young male equines and today is solely applied to them.

## Gelding

When a colt is sexually mature it either becomes a sexually active stallion or is castrated and becomes a gelding. The word *geld* is an old Scandinavian term meaning "barren." Hence a gelding is "one who is made barren."

## Bronco

In Western movies we often hear a cowboy reference to a "bucking bronco." This is due to Mexican influence, the name *bronco* coming from an old Spanish word for something rough—the bronco was originally a half-broken horse that was rough to handle.

## Hack

This name, referring to a horse that is for hire or used for simple riding work, comes to us from France. The French word *haquenée* meant a horse that only ambled along and was used largely by ladies. This type of animal was often employed to pull coaches and was frequently overworked and overused, hence our terms a "hackneyed phrase" and "a hack writer." It was usually a horse of only moderate quality, not suited to hunting, war, or other more specialized activities.

### Thoroughbred

This is the term we use today for a horse with a pedigree—one with the names of its sire and dam in the General Stud Book. Originally such an animal was known simply as a "bred-horse" and was contrasted with a "cocktail" (a contraction of "a cock-tailed horse"), meaning an equine with a docked tail that stood up like the tail of a cockerel. Horses employed for hunting or pulling coaches were the ones that were most likely to have their tails docked in this way and these were also the horses least likely to have a pedigree, hence the connection between cocktails and non-Thoroughbreds. This old equestrian term has given rise to our modern-day name for a mixed drink. Because the horse had mixed parentage and the drink has mixed ingredients, we have called the latter after the former. So, when we drink a cocktail today we are silently paying homage to a mongrel horse with a tail like a cock.

# Why Do We Call a Bad Dream a Nightmare?

If we called a bad dream a nightfright it would be easy to understand, but why a night*mare?* What does it have to do with a female horse?

Very little, is the short answer. In this context, the word *mare* comes from the Anglo-Saxon and means evil spirit or incubus. The incubus was an unpleasant demon who visited sleeping women and sat on their chests, nearly suffocating them. More specifically he was a demon lover who ravished his victims as they twitched and choked in agonized slumber. The resultant offspring, it was said, were often misshapen. Witches welcomed him, innocent girls dreaded him. Viewed with a more objective, practical, modern eye, his exploits doubtless helped to explain embarrassing pregnancies or justified the disposal of deformed babies.

Nocturnal writhings and dreams of erotic assault, caused by intense sexual frustration, could also be explained away as reactions to his unwanted attentions. The sexual nature of nightmares was understood long ago. Writing in 1621 Robert Burton commented, "Maids and widows were particularly subject to terrible dreams in the night, a symptom of melancholy which can be cured by marriage."

The confusion of the demon "mare" with the female

horse "mare" seems to stem from paintings produced two hundred years ago by the Swiss artist Fuseli. They show a sleeping woman with a demon squatting on her chest while through her bedroom curtains there peers the head of a sinister blind horse. The paintings are entitled *Nightmare*. In their day the Fuseli pictures became famous and were produced endlessly as etchings. The staring, blind horse became the "mare" of the nightmare. Whether this was Fuseli merely playing with words or whether he had a more complicated idea behind his imagery is hard to say, but art critics have assumed the latter. Said one, "The horse with its phosphorescent eyes may be the mare on which the incubus rides through the air, apart from being a timeless symbol of virile sexuality."

This misleading association seems to have led to the idea that people suffering from bad dreams are being haunted by horrific, nocturnal demon-horses, when in reality the equine connection is irrelevant.

# Why Were Horses Often Said to Be Hag-ridden?

In earlier times when many superstitions surrounded the keeping of horses, it was often feared that they might fall prey to the attentions of witches. These evil women, it was believed, entered the stables during the night and stole the horses to ride away to their secret coven meetings. The old hags rode them so far and so furiously through the night that they completely exhausted them. By the time they returned them to their stalls—just before dawn—the animals were covered in sweat and suffering from breathing difficulties. Found like this by the stablemen in the morning, there was no doubt what had happened and some unfortunate old woman living nearby would soon find herself persecuted yet again. It was easy to lay the blame against evil forces in this way and to explain the poor condition of the horses as the result of being "hag-ridden," but there was, of course, a much simpler explanation. Early stables were often poorly designed. Security was given precedence over health, and the compartments were frequently designed without any windows. After a long night shut up in the stagnant air, with a serious lack of oxygen, the wretched animals were found in the morning to be drained of energy and bathed in sweat. The wickedness of witches was in reality the stupidity of the stablemen.